THE GEORGIAN GROUP BOOK OF
The Georgian House

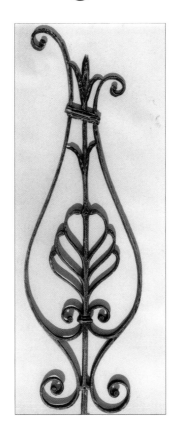

THE GEORGIAN GROUP BOOK OF

The Georgian House

STEVEN PARISSIEN

Foreword by HM Queen Elizabeth The Queen Mother
Introduction by HRH The Duke of Gloucester

AURUM PRESS

For Kit

First published 1995 by Aurum Press Limited, 25 Bedford Avenue, London WC1B 3AT

ISBN 1 85410 370 9

2 4 6 8 10 9 7 5 3 1
1996 1998 1999 1997 1995

Designed by Robert Updegraff
Printed in Singapore by CS Graphics

Frontispiece: Oak-grained sash windows and mellow London stock brickwork on a development of the 1720s, Princelet Street in London's Spitalfields.

Contents

Foreword

Since 1937 The Georgian Group has endeavoured, with much
success, to increase the public's awareness of the value of the
heritage which has descended to us from an age extending from
the reign of King George I to that of King George IV, and spanning
nearly the whole of the eighteenth century and the early part of
the nineteenth.

A lot has been done to enhance the appreciation of Georgian
buildings and to emphasise the need for preserving them. There is,
however, no cause for complacency and the campaign to educate
people, private and professional, must be pursued. *The Book of the
Georgian House* is designed to instruct and at the same time to
entertain. It fulfils these tasks admirably and as Patron of The
Georgian Group I welcome this invaluable guide to a period in
our history in which architecture flourished so notably.

HM Queen Elizabeth The Queen Mother

Introduction

It is hard to believe that my father's generation was brought up to believe that Georgian architecture was dull and repetitive.

For almost sixty years The Georgian Group has worked hard to overcome the prejudices by identifying the heroes of Georgian design, and demonstrating the harmony that Georgian building practices have brought to our towns and cities. The battle to preserve the best of Georgian qualities is never finally won, but this book should help the many people who admire our Georgian legacy to react appropriately, when the forces of expediency threaten those features that are so valued. The harmony, the proportions, the structural details in a language of building that can, all too easily, be mispronounced or wrongly constructed, can only be preserved by understanding and observation. This book is the key to both and I therefore wish it well.

HRH The Duke of Gloucester

Acknowledgements

This book is based on the series of Georgian Group advisory leaflets I produced while Education Secretary at the Group between 1988 and 1992. The messages of the original leaflets were intended to be clear, simple and, where necessary, forceful. As a result, this text does include some repetition of some of the most salient historical and conservation lessons; however, they are all points – such as the Georgians' horror of unpainted pine – which benefit from a good deal of repetition today.

There are many experts who helped check and advise on the original series of Georgian Group leaflets. There is not the space to list them all; however, I am particularly indebted to the following individuals for their help and guidance: Susan Anstruther, Patrick Baty, Ian Bristow, Neil Burton, Oran Campbell, Dan Cruickshank, John Fidler, William Hawkes, Philip Heath, Charles Hind, Arnold Root, Treve Rosoman, Chris Salmond, Kit Wedd, Annabel Westman, Robert Weston and Rory Young.

I would also like to thank all those who have kindly opened their homes to Ian Parry's expert photography, most notably John Cordle, Dan Cruickshank, Geoffrey Morley, Duncan Wilson and the late Sir Philip Shelbourne. Thanks too to Martin Drury of The National Trust, Charles Brooking and Caroline Reed of The Brooking Collection, and Christopher Woodward of The Building of Bath Museum for allowing Ian to photograph.

Lastly, I would like to single out for special thanks my resourceful commissioning editor, Piers Burnett of Aurum Press; Robert Updegraff, the most helpful and genial of designers; my agent, Sara Menguc of Murray Pollinger, who originally placed this book; the staff and Executive Committee of The Georgian Group, for their support and advice; and especially The Monument Trust, whose generous funding made possible both my Georgian Group appointment and the original series of advisory leaflets.

DR STEVEN PARISSIEN
LONDON, DECEMBER 1994

* * *

THE GEORGIAN GROUP was founded in 1937 to save Georgian buildings, monuments, parks and gardens from destruction or disfigurement, and to encourage their appropriate repair or restoration. The Group largely depends on members' subscriptions to finance its work; it is a registered charity (no. 209934), and benefits from covenants. To join, or to obtain further information about the work and activities of the Group, write to them at 6 Fitzroy Square, London W1P 6DX.

THE HOUSE

The Georgian House

EVERYONE LOVES A Georgian house. There is something in its grandeur, its materials and above all in its fine proportions which intrinsically appeals to nearly all of us.

And everyone thinks they know what a Georgian house should look like. However, determining exactly what is meant by the term 'Georgian' is often more difficult than it first appears. It is helpful, then, to define that catch-all term 'Georgian' before we begin. Politically speaking, the Georgian period began in 1714 – the year in which King George I of Hanover succeeded to the British throne left vacant on the death of the last of the Stuarts, Queen Anne. The period can end in 1830, the year in which George IV died – or possibly in 1837, when William IV, George IV's younger brother and heir, died without a legitimate successor (while bequeathing the nation a series of bastards by his mistress Mrs Jordan). The Georgian period thus covers the reigns of the four Georges: George I (1714–27), his son George II (1727–60), his grandson George III (1760–1820, a reign which encompasses Prince George's celebrated Regency of 1811–20) and George IV (1820–30). Onto this can be appended the short reign of William IV (1830–7); the Victorian period properly started only with the accession of Queen Victoria herself in 1837.

While the visual arts tend to borrow the nomenclature of politics, however, they can rarely be fastened as securely in the same chronological straitjacket. In architecture, for example, it is naive as well as misleading to attribute certain styles and forms to a particular reign, as if that style ceased to be practised immediately on a particular monarch's death. Artistic development is often closely tied to political fortunes; nevertheless, the idea that stylistic 'periods' begin and end at neatly defined times is false. Moreover, the idea that what appeared on the streets of London or Philadelphia – or indeed in the pages of the latest pattern-books – was instantly taken up in every county or state in the land is illusory. Provincial craftsmen continued to work in tried and

ABOVE: *Detail of a Late Georgian door from The Brooking Collection.*

OPPOSITE: *A house from Fournier Street in east London's Spitalfields district, an area developed during the 1720s and 30s to house the new influx of Huguenot immigrants from France. The swept-head ground floor windows are recessed, in accordance with the capital's 18th-century fire regulations; those on the first and second floors, however, are virtually flush with the masonry, and have most of their sash boxes exposed.*

11

trusted ways long after the styles and manners they had learned from their fore-fathers had become very old-fashioned by metropolitan standards. Thus provincial craftsman-ship which from the evidence of the pattern-books of the day looks like work of, say, 1720 may in fact date from thirty, forty or even fifty years later.

Yet although precisely defined 'periods' can prove very misleading, it is worth try-ing to establish some artificial chronological boundaries in order to define what can otherwise end up as a very nebulous series of stylistic developments. In fact the politi-cal parameters of the Georgian period – i.e. the years from 1714 to 1830 – are surpris-ingly useful. The accession of George I in 1714 roughly corresponds to the advent of the 'Palladian' style – a return to the philosophy and proportions of Ancient Roman Classicism, whose precepts and forms dominated the architectural world for the remainder of the century. The reign of the first of the Hanoverian kings also neatly corresponds to the ascendancy of the so-called 'Whig oligarchy', the establishment of which gave Britain unprecedented political stability at the expense of political and social reforms. By the time George I died in 1727 the Whig party was well entrenched in government – so much so that the accession of George II made no difference what-soever to the premiership of Sir Robert Walpole. Indeed, the Whigs were to remain in power, largely uninterrupted, for the next sixty years. Georgian architecture should not, however, be seen as the physical expression of the Whig creed. Acknowledged Tories and likely independents played just as much a part in the evolution of the Georgian house as did the 'Whig' patrons. It has recently been alleged, for example, that even the godfather of Palladianism, the 3rd Earl of Burlington, was in truth not a Whig at all, but in secret a rabid, reactionary Jacobite.

At the latter end of the Georgian era, 1830 serves as an equally useful boundary between Georgians and Victorians as 1714 does between Baroque and Palladian, Tory and Whig. The years after 1830 saw great political upheavals, most notably with the passage of the Great Reform Act of 1832. In Britain, the last of George III's numerous sons – George IV and William IV – died during the 1830s. In America the last of the Founding Fathers expired: Jefferson had already gone in 1826, to be followed by Monroe in 1831 and Madison in 1836. Architecturally, too, the 1830s witnessed a great sea change in style. Ending the hegemony of austere Neoclassicism were a whole series of exuberant revivals and reinterpretations – Italianate, Gothic, Elizabethan, Egyptian, Louis XVI, even Saxon and Norman. Experimentation with a more academic medievalism laid the foundations for the full-blooded Gothic revival-ism of the 1840s, and sounded the death-knell for the habitual (and, it must be said, by this time rather dull) style of domestic Classicism. Pugin's *Contrasts* of 1836 cruelly laid bare the wafer-thin shams on which much Georgian design and construction were based, calling for a robust and honest Gothicism to take the place of the out-moded and discredited Classical tradition. Polemics such as Pugin's helped to inaugu-rate the muscular and self-confident age of the Victorians, and served to make the confused, diverse and eclectic 1830s into something of a watershed in the development of architectural and decorative design. For these reasons the year 1830 can serve as a useful shorthand.

It is important, though, to make further subdivisions of the Georgian era in order to prevent the term 'Georgian' from becoming wholly meaningless. A 'Georgian' house can date from 1720 or from 1820; yet these houses can differ substantially in the

methods of construction, the types of materials used, and the finishes and furnishings with which they were provided. Thus, to help clarify the general stylistic developments, it is useful to split the Georgian period into three sub-sections, roughly corresponding to the supremacy of the Palladian style (c.1714–60), of the Adam or Neoclassical style (c.1760–90) and of the Regency or, as it was known in America, the Federal style (c.1790–1830).

These distinctions are inevitably highly generalized and approximate. They can, however, help to dispel a few popular misconceptions as to what a 'Georgian' house really is. One of the most common of these is the confusion over exactly when the 'Regency' period was, and how 'Regency' design relates to that of the 'Georgian' era. In the visual arts, at least, 'Regency' is synonymous with 'Late Georgian'. Yet in political terms the Regency – i.e. the years during which Prince George (King George IV after 1820) acted as Regent for his increasingly mad and blind father, George III – only covers the nine years from 1811 to 1820. We should beware, then, of interchanging political and architectural terminology too often and too glibly.

In America, things become even more confusing, since, for obvious reasons, British historical labels do not always apply on the other side of the Atlantic. For example, in America the 'Georgian' or 'Colonial' period comes to an abrupt halt with the Declaration of Independence in 1776, and the period following this is usually dignified by the term 'Federal' – a label which embraces both the Adamesque style imported into the new United States during the 1780s and 90s and the more robust, Regency-style forms which became fashionable in the early 19th century. The more austere Greek Revival style of the 1820s and 30s can be called 'Jeffersonian', while the French term 'Empire' (whose artistic boundaries far exceed the eleven years (1804–15) of Napoleon's French

Rosalind Hudson's splendid wooden models of typical Bath houses chart the development of the urban facade during the Georgian period. From the left: 14 Gay Street of 1755; 9 Cavendish Place of 1808–16 (sited on a hill, which accounts for the building's ramped cornices and string-courses); and 9 Cleveland Place West, of c.1829, with its fashionable, Soaneian incised decoration.

13

RIGHT: *Elfreth's Alley in Philadelphia. Although the street was first laid out in 1702, most of these houses date from the mid-1720s or later.*

FAR RIGHT: *Houses from Boston's Beacon Hill district, developed during the first years of the 19th century. Decoration of these elevations was deliberately kept to a minimum; they were left as plain brick facades, with few stone dressings and no covering of stucco.*

BELOW: *A detail from Eldon Square in Newcastle. These strong, stone-fronted Neoclassical facades were designed by local architect John Dobson and built between 1825 and 1831 as part of speculative builder Richard Grainger's ambitious and visionary schemes to redevelop the city. On his death in 1861, Grainger himself was called 'one of the greatest architects of his age'. This did not, however, prevent Newcastle City Council from demolishing all but a fragment of the square in 1969 in one of the most inexplicable acts of municipal vandalism since the war.*

Empire) can be used for the continentally inspired decorative features which became increasingly common in the United States after the War of 1812–14. For the sake of brevity, however, the term 'Georgian' is used throughout this book to signify the architecture and decoration of the approximate period 1714–1830, both in Britain and in America.

Today Georgian buildings are universally revered and admired. The British Government itself persists in demanding less stringent conditions for the statutory protection (the 'listing') of buildings built before 1840. However, while there has always been a large degree of public affection for Georgian buildings, this has not always been reflected in official policy. At the end of the 19th century, for example, important Georgian buildings were being demolished wholesale, and after World War I the pace of demolition actually quickened. While the Bishop of London was frustrated in his horrific proposal of 1919 to demolish nineteen of Wren and Hawksmoor's incomparable churches, in the ensuing two decades many fine Georgian townscapes – most notably Georgian Bloomsbury, Adam's Adelphi and Nash's Regent Street – were systematically destroyed. During the 1930s many of the capital's finest squares were also decimated, among them key London landmarks such as Portman, Cavendish, Berkeley and Mecklenburgh Squares. As Gavin Stamp wrote in 1982, the great Georgian houses of London's West End proved to be as vulnerable as the neighbouring middle-class terraces: 'Devonshire House came down in 1924, Dorchester House in 1929, Chesterfield House in 1935 and Norfolk House in 1938. Lansdowne House was mutilated and spoiled in 1934.'

It was a proposal to demolish Nash's splendid and irreplaceable Carlton House Terrace which finally led to the foundation of The Georgian Group in 1937. This new, vociferous pressure group pledged to fight against the tide of demolition. As Lord Derwent, one of the founders of the Group, told the House of Lords in December 1936:

> The 18th century and the Regency time gave the most glorious architectural heritage to the country. Having the privilege of enjoying these beauties, we did nothing to ensure that the privilege should be handed down to our successors. Instead, we were replacing these buildings with others, the majority of which were jerry-built, shoddy and an agony to the eye.

The newly formed Georgian Group faced an uphill struggle against numerous vested interests and considerable official philistinism. Inevitably, victories were not won every week; much of Georgian Bloomsbury, for example, was razed to make way for London University – despite Nancy Mitford's quixotic offer to chain herself naked to the railings in order to frustrate the demolition contractors. However, the Group did manage to save many fine Georgian buildings from unnecessary destruction: important Georgian survivors such as London's Abingdon Street (tragically destroyed by German bombs a few years later) and Nash's Regent's Park terraces.

Pressure for development was even keener after 1945, and architectural atrocities continued unabated throughout the 1950s and 60s. However, by the early 1970s the conservationists were, if not exactly gaining the upper hand, then at least helping to change both public and official opinion regarding the merits of our surviving Georgian heritage. The Town and Country Planning Acts of 1968 and 1971 introduced

The sweeping, stuccoed colonnade of John Nash's Park Crescent of 1812–22. Built as part of Nash's grandiose Regent's Park scheme, these houses were substantially rebuilt (retaining the same elevations) in the 1960s.

15

the concept of listing – affording genuine protection for Britain's valuable buildings – while in 1974 local authorities were exhorted to appoint Conservation Officers to promote the new doctrine of architectural conservation. By the 1980s even former villains were being persuaded to change their ways. Bath City Council, for example, finally abandoned its policy of demolishing valuable working-class Georgian housing and began to treat it with the same respect accorded to the city's more famous monuments and streets. The fruits of the conservationists' campaigns can be seen all over the country; today, for example, what remains of Georgian Bath has been rightly designated a World Heritage Site.

In America, too, the tide has turned, with Federal bodies such as The National Trust for Historic Preservation and the National Parks Service, and regional organizations such as The Society for the Preservation of New England Antiquities, taking a strong lead in ensuring that the country's surviving Georgian and Federal homes are not only conserved, but restored in an authentic and appropriate manner. Indeed, in many ways – particularly in the study and re-creation of original interiors – the conservation movement in the US is far in advance of its transatlantic cousins. There is still, for example, no real equivalent in Britain to the splendid array of highly accessible guides produced by the American National Trust's publishing arm, The Preservation Press. Hopefully this book will go some way to correcting this imbalance.

Impressively wide bays, relieving arches over the ground floor windows and stuccoed pilasters, linking first and attic floors, distinguish this handsome house on the summit of Boston's Beacon Hill. Built in 1800, 85 Mount Vernon Hill was Harrison Otis' second house in the district; he also owned a striking mansion of 1796 at the bottom of the hill, in Cambridge Street. Otis, a prominent lawyer, made his fortune developing Beacon Hill after 1795, and subsequently served both in the Federal Congress and as Mayor of Boston.

Due to the efforts of the conservation lobby in both Britain and America, and to a growing awareness of the importance of our architectural heritage, the wholesale demolition of Georgian buildings is today a thing of the past. However, this should not be a cause for complacency. Countless Georgian or Colonial buildings are still very much at risk; indeed, despite the lip service currently paid to historic structures, old buildings, and particularly their interiors, are still regularly treated in a cavalier or dismissive manner, the familiar claim that traditional styles and forms are simply being reinterpreted in a modern manner being all too often used to mask the removal of all historic character.

Good restoration relies on sympathy and sensitivity and, above all, on the ability to leave something alone when it looks right and is doing its job. Unsurprisingly, sympathetic refurbishment can often work out far cheaper than heavy-handed over-restoration. Good restoration can transform an old house from a shabby, dilapidated or neglected building – or from a characterless, modernized and 'streamlined' shell – into an appealing, visually appropriate and extremely comfortable home that is also a sound financial investment. Bad restoration, on the other hand, can not only look hideous or ridiculous, but can also damage the fabric of the house; such structural harm, when combined with the effect of making the building less of a genuinely 'period' home, inevitably reduces the value of the property and makes it harder to sell.

At the same time, it is useful to bear in mind that, while your refurbishment or repair may quite rightly seek to recapture much of the spirit and historic character of your old home, it can be rather dangerous to go too far down the path of authenticity. The modern obsession with what John Betjeman termed 'antiquarian prejudice' – removing features merely because they do not correspond to a suitably ancient period or date – does little for the house: attempting to return the whole of the house to some mythical, overly precise yesteryear generally ends in failure. Not only may there be very little evidence to support the 'restoration' – and indeed very few craftsmen able to execute the work even if a precedent was discovered – but, to follow William Morris' eminently sensible Victorian doctrine, all new work that is done in order to 'return' the house to 1720, 1820 or even 1920 will inevitably be just that: new, and not original. As Jane Nylander has recently written:

A mid-18th-century door panel, in wood but with a composition ornament, from The Brooking Collection. This fine example has had its paint layers removed to reveal the clogged details of the intricate mouldings. However, paint always needs to be applied to joinery or panelling such as this; without the protection it affords damage can easily occur, particularly in today's centrally heated homes. This piece has already suffered some damage.

> A common mistake in the restoration of historic interiors is to . . . arbitrarily select a date for restoration (often the date of the original construction of the building) and then look for beautiful designs and materials appropriate to that date. Some of the interiors created by this procedure would probably astonish their original owners.

Careful, sympathetic restoration can actually make your old home look far more beautiful and inviting than trying to drag the building back to some semi-fictitious past. And it is often true that spending less on refurbishment can produce better results than throwing money at an old building: so many historic homes are ruined through wholesale 'restorations' which, while undoubtedly well-intentioned, are often sadly misguided.

One of the primary purposes of this book is to demonstrate that there *are* good practical reasons, as well as aesthetic considerations, for approaching restoration and repair in the right way. These arguments, together with historical summaries and suggestions for maintenance and repair, you will find detailed in the following chapters.

2

Georgian Style

T HE KEY TO Georgian Classicism is not, as is often thought, individual elements of the classical vocabulary. Pediments, columns or pilasters do not in themselves constitute a Georgian building – a mistake the purveyors of sham-Georgian continue to make today.

The true determinant of Georgian architecture, no matter how grand or modest in scale, is the principle of proportion: the proportion of each individual facade, of wall space to window space, of room height to room length, and so on. 'Proportion is the first Principle, and proper Appropriation of the parts constitute Symmetry and Harmony,' wrote Robert Morris, English Palladianism's first published theorist, in 1751. Geometric proportions – as propounded in the Italian pattern-books of Palladio and Serlio and as executed in the works of Inigo Jones – were, early Georgians such as Morris believed, the means by which true perfection of form could be attained in every-day life. Realizing the mathematical ideals of architecture would, it was hoped, allow designers to mirror the 'ideal beauty' of Nature itself, a goal much propounded by the philosophers of the late 17th and early 18th centuries.

Simple, disciplined proportion could thus provide the key to perfection. In one of his earliest works, the *Lectures* of 1734, Robert Morris devised a 'Universal Rule' to 'serve for all manner of Rooms whatever'. His scheme of seven basic proportions – based on those of Palladio and, ultimately, of Plato – was anchored in the most elemental geometric shapes: a square, a circle, a cube, a cube-and-a-half, and so on. The cube-and-a-half proportion proved particularly adaptable to domestic construction; many humble Georgian terraced facades were built according to this manner, the square or cube providing the measurement for the first, second and attic floors, the half-square the guide for the ground floor.

It is deeply ironic that what is popularly regarded as the best-loved and the most quintessentially British period of architecture actually derived its inspiration directly

ABOVE: *No. 61 Green Street, Mayfair, London, built by Roger Morris in 1730 as his own home. The simple, cubic proportions of the facade not only mirror Morris' country house designs, but also reflect those propounded by his kinsman Robert Morris in his Lectures (1734).*

OPPOSITE: *The Blue Velvet Room at Chiswick House, Middlesex, built by the 3rd Earl of Burlington in the late 1720s. The room was the centrepiece of the house, epitomizing Early Palladian taste.*

19

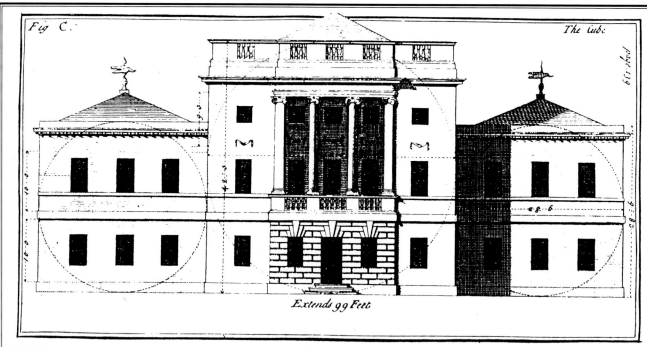

Fig. C.   The Cube

Extends 99 Feet

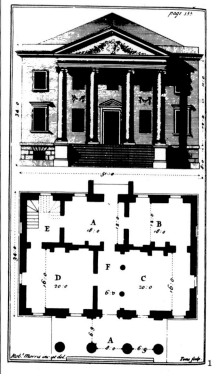

page 155

A   B
E
D   F   C

Robt Morris inv et del.   Toms sculp.

13

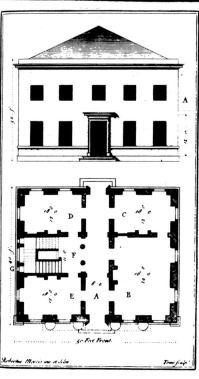

A

D   C
F
G
E   A   B

50 Feet Front

Robertus Morris inv et delin.   Toms sculp.

14

C

B

Robertus Morris inv et delin.   Toms sculp.

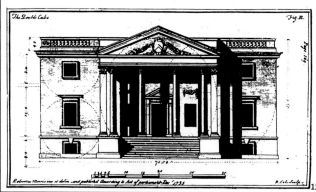

The Double Cube   Fig. D.

Robertus Morris inv et delin. and published according to Act of parliament Dec. 1735.   B. Cole Sculp.

12

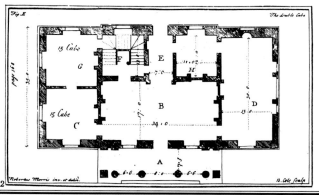

Fig. E.   The Double Cube

15 Cube   G   F   E   H
                    B   D
15 Cube   C

A

Robertus Morris inv et delin.   B. Cole Sculp.

from Italy, a land despised by the Georgians as the home of the Papal Anti-Christ and the Counter-Reformation. Soon after the accession of George I to the British throne in 1714, the 3rd Earl of Burlington led a reaction against the indiscipline of the Baroque school, promoting an architectural style based on the forms and philosophy of the Ancient Roman architect Marcus Vitruvius Pollio, as interpreted by the 16th-century architect Andrea Palladio, Palladio's Italian contemporaries and the 17th-century English genius Inigo Jones (a far more politically acceptable progenitor than Palladio himself). The application of 'Palladian' theories and forms to British buildings in the late 1710s and 20s effectively launched what we now call 'Georgian Classicism'. It was this Italian-influenced movement which formed the basis of British domestic design not only during the Georgian period but also far beyond.

By 1730 the would-be architect, builder, patron or houseowner had at his or her disposal an increasingly comprehensive array of helpful pattern-books to use as design guides or as aids to measurement. As architectural historian Eileen Harris has written:

> Starting in 1724 with Halfpenny's *Practical Architecture*, a succession of books appeared over the next decade or so offering . . . simple methods of determining the diameter of the column (i.e. the module) or of proportioning the entire order . . . which in turn were extrapolated from Palladio, Vignola and Scamozzi.

The most successful of these new guides was architect James Gibbs' *Book of Architecture* of 1728. This proved highly influential not only in Britain but also in the American colonies, Gibbsian designs and motifs appearing in great profusion in American cities throughout the next century. Gibbs was in turn plagiarized by subsequent authors: as

ABOVE: *Elevation of 33 Northampton Street, Bath, drawn by Ceredig Williams for The Building of Bath Museum. The geometrical overlay demonstrates the simple proportions of a typical mid-Georgian house, and the manner in which these proportions – in this case, largely derived from the humble square – corresponded to the Classical orders.*

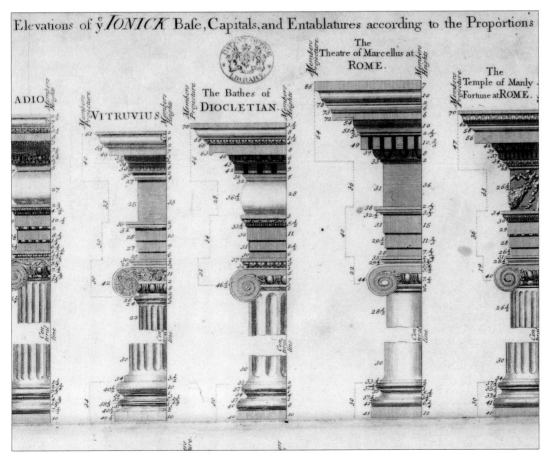

Elevations of ÿ *IONICK* Base, Capitals, and Entablatures according to the Proportions

ADIO · VITRUVIUS · The Bathes of DIOCLETIAN. · The Theatre of Marcellus at ROME. · The Temple of Manly Fortune at ROME.

OPPOSITE: *Three illustrations from Robert Morris' Lectures, lessons in Palladian aesthetics published in 1734 and, with new additions, in 1739. The proportions of all these designs are based on simple cubes.*

LEFT: *Comparative, intricately measured Ionic orders, culled by Batty Langley from a variety of ancient and Renaissance authorities for his City and Country Builder's and Workman's Treasury of Designs of 1740. This type of helpful study saved architects, builders and their clients the bother of consulting original sources for the correct proportions.*

Eileen Harris observes, the *Book of Architecture*'s 'exceptionally large number and variety of details was a feasting ground for compilers like Langley, Salmon, Hoppus and Oakley, whose popular builders' manuals disseminated copies to workmen who could not afford Gibbs' folio.' Of these authors, Batty Langley was by far the most prolific, publishing over twenty conventionally Palladian pattern-books and builders' guides between 1726 and his death in 1751.

During the Georgian era both urban and rural homes continued to be disposed according to the strict Palladian principles of proportion, as expounded in print by pattern-book authors such as Gibbs, Morris and Langley. As time progressed, however, these high-flown theories were modified by more practical considerations. The availability of new building materials – a direct result of the rapid advance of industrialization in Britain – certainly helped to define the form of the average home as much as did the thoughts of Palladio or Jones or the pragmatic reinterpretations of Batty Langley. At the same time, the tightening of building regulations (see chapter 3, below) did much to govern the development of what we now regard as the typical 'Georgian' house.

The austere Greek Neoclassicism of Holland, Hope and their followers – all the rage for interior decorators by 1810 – made relatively little difference to the overall style of the run-of-the-mill exterior, although isolated Greek motifs such as the acroterion (often reduced simply to plaster quarter-circle 'ears' adorning the doorcase or roof) or a Greek key pattern, perhaps incised into the stucco, did indicate some superficial Neoclassical influence. The principal developments in the later 18th-century domestic facade – larger windows, simpler doorcases, stuccoed brickwork – were generally the result of technological advance or popular whim, more than a sincere devotion to the forms of the antique world. Nash's or Cubitt's vast new estates of the 1820s were not, in their outward form, so markedly different from their predecessors of the 1720s: rectangular or perhaps round-headed sash windows dominated uniform, flat-roofed and highly symmetrical terrace houses.

Materials were, though, just as important as the question of style in determining the direction of Georgian Classicism, at least so far as the average house was concerned. Again, this is a factor which modern manufacturers of pseudo-Georgiana have failed to appreciate. No amount of flat, flimsy fakery will turn a modern brick and concrete box into a Georgian home; only by using authentic and appropriate materials can we attempt to match the philosophical approach and the constructional methods of the Georgians.

The changes wrought by the Industrial Revolution in the 18th and early 19th centuries made particularly lasting contributions to design and construction. Even the most basic of building materials, brick, was profoundly affected by technological advances. Brick kilns were increasingly fired not with traditional fuels such as wood, charcoal or bracken, but with coal – the fuel of industrialization. This allowed kilns to attain higher temperatures than previously, which in turn enabled a greater range of brick colours to be produced: the colour was now determined not only by the colour of the clay but also by the temperature of the firing. (In 1756 Isaac Ware noted that 'the degree of burning makes a considerable difference in the condition of the bricks, but their principal distinction is from the nature of the materials with which they are

The south side of Bedford Square, London. Begun in 1775, this represented a conscious attempt to realize the Palladian ideal in a middle-class urban context. Greater prominence is given to the centrepiece (which, unusually, is of six and not five or three bays) by providing it not only with a pediment but also with a striking veneer of painted stucco. Note that, while most of the first floor windows to the west of the centrepiece (those on the right) have been extended down to floor level, those to the east retain their original proportions.

made.') No longer had architects and builders to rely wholly on the ubiquitous 'hot' red brick which characterized the brick buildings of the late 17th century. Bricks could now be made that were brown, yellow, grey, white or cream in colour – a development which married well with changing aesthetic tastes. The middle classes looking to buy a house wanted a reflection of their new-found wealth which was as opulent and up-to-date as possible. To them, red brickwork was far too redolent of old-fashioned values and of the humble dwellings of past decades, and since the grandest homes were now built in the best Palladian manner – that is, faced in stone – they wanted the next best thing: brickwork that was coloured or finished to resemble expensive stonework. Hence the sudden popularity of stone-coloured bricks, which avoided the stigma of being associated with last year's fashion.

One of the most obviously Italianate of Georgian building fashions was the sudden popularity from the early 1770s onwards of 'stucco' finishes. Stucco was essentially a thin render – a mixture based principally on lime and sand – which could be applied to a wall in three coats in an attempt to disguise inferior masonry as finely dressed blocks of ashlar. Originated by the Romans and much used by their Italian descendants, it also became the hallmark of the Late Georgian terrace. It was in essence simply an imitative material – like graining or marbling, those other popular illusory devices beloved of Georgian designers.

24

At the same time, in response to advances in glass technology, windows were coming to occupy more and more of the wall space. The larger panes of glass that could now be made were strong enough to be introduced into the sash window format without any need for a complex grid of wooden or metal supports. By the 1770s it was the height of fashion to lower the sills of first floor windows and to fit larger sashes in the enlarged spaces; the 1776 building contract for Bedford Square, for example, included the provision that 'liberty [was] to be given to cut down any of the windows so low as the floors of the rooms.'

Developments in the iron industry, too, were revolutionizing the manner in which the Georgian or Federal house was built in the last decades of the 18th century. Iron girders allowed designers to throw out cantilevered staircases or balconies in seemingly unsupported fashion from the walls; iron window frames enabled window sizes to be increased, and glazing bar profiles made thinner; iron beams helped to reduce the amount of constructional timber, while iron plates gave added protection against fire. It was thus as much the technological developments and new inventions brought by industrial growth as the whims of the celebrated arbiters of style that shaped the average Georgian home.

The surviving range of Mecklenburgh Square, London, built between 1810 and 1821 by Joseph Kay. The rest of the square became a casualty of interwar architectural vandalism.

3

The British House

W HILE NEW STYLISTIC influences and newly available building materials were clearly instrumental to the appearance of the Georgian house, legislation, too, played its part in determining the development of domestic Georgian Classicism.

During the years following the Great Fire of London of 1666 a number of tough building regulations were imposed in order to control unscrupulous speculators and dishonest builders. The 1667 Buildings Act attempted to ensure that future buildings in the capital were to be as sound – and, most importantly, as fireproof – as possible, and that the pavements that bordered them were to be as secure as possible. The Act stipulated that brick or stone, and not inflammable timber, was to be used for the facades of buildings, a measure strengthened in 1707, when external wooden cornices were banned, and again in 1709, when sash boxes were ordered to be recessed at least four inches from the outer face of the principal elevation. Like its predecessors, the 1709 Act was only aimed at buildings in London; however, it was generally the rule that where the capital led, the other towns and cities of Britain's empire followed – albeit some years afterwards.

A measure that applied to the whole of the country was the most comprehensive and effective of all: the Building Act of 1774. Drafted by architects Robert Taylor and George Dance, the Act aimed to end jerry-building by defining the four types or 'rates' of house which could be built in future. Each rate had its own, well-defined limits. The First Rate house was worth over £850 a year in ground rent, occupying more than 900 square feet of space; at the other end of the scale, the Fourth Rate was a house worth less than £150 a year, which occupied less than 350 square feet. And within each category was a list of specific building requirements (including the stipulation that all external window joinery was to be hidden behind the outer skin of masonry as a precaution against fire).

ABOVE: *A Third Rate Regency house in London's Albany Street, with one of the most characteristic of Regency motifs: a fine, iron-and-lead balcony.*

OPPOSITE: *Simple, early Georgian facades in London's Bedford Row, with exposed sash boxes, gauged brick window arches and, typically for London, evidence of post-war rebuilding.*

27

First, Second and Fourth rates of housing, according to the Building Act of 1774, as realized by Alison Shepherd for the second edition of John Summerson's masterly overview of Georgian London *(Barrie and Jenkins, 1988).*

The 1774 Act certainly helped to stem – although it by no means eradicated – much of the poor-quality building of the period. However, it also led to inevitable standardization which, when translated to the late 18th-century terraces of London or Dublin, could in visual terms prove increasingly dull – an effect that Summerson so memorably termed the 'inexpressible monotony of the typical London street' (or, more graphically, 'one damn Georgian building after another'). At the same time, while the Act was meant to be constructive and helpful, and conducive to good building practice, to many builders and craftsmen it represented an unwarranted interference in their traditional trades. Its reception was further worsened by the punitive legislation designed by the governments of the day to raise revenue. The extension of the hated Window Tax of 1696 to include all homes with seven or more windows in 1766 and six or more in 1784, and the implementation of the Brick Tax of 1784 (a measure designed expressly to help pay for the recent, ruinous American war), served to cancel out many of the improvements effected in the construction of average homes by the 1774 Act.

The fact that legislation such as the 1774 Act was needed underlines the pace of building development during the Georgian era. Streets, crescents, squares, even whole new towns sprang up with increasing regularity as the 18th century progressed, so that by the end of the century many areas of Britain or America were completely unrecognizable from their aspect in 1714. The great majority of these developments were built according to the speculative building system which had evolved after the Great Fire of

London. A builder-speculator bought the leasehold of a site from the ground land-lord, and then proceeded to build only the basic rudiments of the house or terrace. As Dan Cruickshank has noted:

> The object of the builder, after acquiring his building lease, was to erect the shell of a building, roofed and floored and usually with the bare internal walls roughly plastered out, and sell it on before ground rent became payable.

The first true occupier of the house would then have the carcass finished to his or her own taste, leaving the builder-speculator with a tidy profit.

That at any rate was the theory of speculation. In practice, however, things invariably went wrong. All too often inexperienced architects or builders failed to find purchasers for the houses they had erected before the peppercorn rent originally levied by the ground-landlord had expired, and before they had expended large amounts of their own money. A typical example was the architect Roger Morris' speculative venture of 1740 on a piece of land adjacent to London's Westminster Bridge and the Houses of Parliament. The lease was fixed to last for 72 years (an average term for leaseholds of the time), but for the first two years Morris was allowed to rent the site at a peppercorn one shilling a year. However, when this expired in 1742 Morris still had most of the properties on his hands. And in March 1745 he wrote that he was still incurring heavy costs, 'there not being at present any one of the thirteen houses Tenanted in Bridge Street, nor any probability of [them] being Lett'. By the time of Morris' death in 1749 his name was still featuring on the rent roll for Bridge Street and New Palace Yard. At least Morris had not been bankrupted; others, though, were not so lucky. Financial failures due to unsuccessful building speculations were rife in London and the major cities by 1800. Even the illustrious Adam brothers were not

A high-class brick terrace development of 1724: Montpelier Row in Twickenham, Middlesex.

immune. Their Thames-side Adelphi development of 1768–72 was to provide houses designed to be 'remarkably strong and substantial, and finished in the most elegant and complete measure'. But the development was a failure: 3000 workmen were dismissed, and the Adams narrowly escaped financial ruin.

Over-optimistic architects and builders were not the only casualties of the speculative system. So, all too often, were the houses themselves. Builders worried by the threat of financial collapse built rapidly and meanly. As Dan Cruickshank has remarked of the typical London terrace development: 'The well-wrought and fashionably detailed facades are invariably only one brick (four inches) thick,' the lack of structural stability being multiplied 'by the use of softwood timber in brickwork, and lime mortar mixed with street dirt'. Georgian developments were often only designed to last the sixty, seventy, eighty and ninety-nine years of the original lease; it is thus remarkable that so many of them have survived relatively unscathed into the 20th century. It is perhaps only the even shorter life of modern building developments that has made Georgian building practices appear somewhat less heinous.

Not every new house of the Georgian era was, of course, part of a large scale, speculative development. Rural cottages – often built in the same basic manner as they had been for decades, with only a new building material or a more fashionable decorative scheme to distinguish them from similar homes of the preceding century – were still erected in small but steady numbers. However, it is the urban or semi-urban terrace and its derivatives which is the Georgian period's great contribution to historic building types.

The domestic terrace was not a Georgian invention. Inigo Jones had introduced the terrace development of brick and stone-built houses to London's Covent Garden in the 1630s. However, it was only in the years after 1714 that the visual and structural possibilities of the Classical terrace were properly exploited.

Colen Campbell's 31–4 Old Burlington Street, London, begun in 1718, provided the template for countless astylar terraces of the 18th century. Every element of Campbell's facades was in accordance with the strict, Palladian rules of proportion, the windows and doors being sized so as to enable the elevation to conform to Palladio's simple geometric guidelines, and the first floors provided with added emphasis owing to the more elevated functions of the rooms inside. However, by the mid-1720s attempts were being made to design terraces that were not merely sequences of uniform, standardized house units, but more ambitious and stylistically unified compositions. One of the first 'palace-fronted' terraces – that is, terraces emphasized by a central pediment and, perhaps, end projections – was built on the east side of London's Grosvenor Square in 1725. Both this speculation and its contemporaries – of which by far the most successful was Bath's Queen Square – derived their inspiration more from recent experiments such as Henry Aldrich's Peckwater Quad at Christ Church, Oxford (begun in 1707) than from Inigo Jones' famous but monotonous terraces in Covent Garden.

By the middle of the 18th century the classic Georgian terrace was being bent into unconventional shapes. John Wood the Elder's Circus in Bath, begun in 1754, was a bizarre and ambitious, yet in the event highly successful, attempt to combine Palladian planning with a circular context based on Judaic, Druidic and Masonic imagery as well as on more predictable antique sources. However, the credit for inventing the crescent

The ancestor of the Georgian terrace: Henry Aldrich's Peckwater Quad, begun in 1707, at Christ Church, Oxford.

No. 31 Old Burlington Street, London. The simple, Palladian proportions of Burlington's original development are still visible here, yet most of its neighbours have been demolished or irreversibly altered.

Michael Searles' bold composition of The Paragon at Blackheath, in southeast London, built in 1793.

The spectacular, hilltop sweep of John Wood the Younger's Royal Crescent, Bath, of 1767–75. This revolutionary, monumental structure was a milestone in urban planning.

must go to his son. John Wood the Younger's Royal Crescent in Bath (1767–75) was undeniably dramatic, the hillside dominated by the vast sweep of its palace front with its imposing giant Ionic order.

By the end of the century some of the more daring designers were beginning to disrupt the unbroken line of the Georgian terrace. At Gloucester Circus in Greenwich (1790) and, most famously, at The Paragon in nearby Blackheath (1793), Michael Searles divided the terrace into a series of separate but linked compositions: pairs of semi-detached houses were connected by lower, set-back blocks or simply by colonnades. However, John Nash's monumental London terraces of the 1810s and 20s, stretching from Regent's Park to Carlton House, reinforced the supremacy of the unbroken terrace front – albeit using elevations that were now of stuccoed rather than exposed brickwork. This supremacy was to survive well into the Victorian era.

The grandest of all the variants of the consciously planned Georgian terrace was the square. Squares were appearing in London and the other great cities of the Empire by the middle of the 18th century. John Wood's revolutionary, palace-fronted terraces of Queen Square in Bath were begun as early as 1729. Dublin's first planned square, Merrion Square, was begun in 1762. It was only in the auspicious year of 1775, however, that work began on London's first entirely symmetrical square: Bedford Square, completed in 1783. By the 1820s the stuccoed square, with its pilastered elevations and central pediment, was a fundamental prerequisite for any housing development of pretension.

4

The American House

I N MANY WAYS the American house during the Colonial and Federal eras was markedly similar to the British house – the principal difference being that, as in the more distant provinces of Britain, new ideas and concepts took a little longer to arrive. Materials were often different: wood, for example, was far more widely used on the east coast of America than stone, which was rarely found locally (marble or stone floors remained very rare in the US before the 19th century). But the basic principles on which the Georgian home was built, as well as the manner in which it was equipped and furnished, remained roughly the same on both sides of the Atlantic.

For much of the 18th century the typically modest Colonial style of the 17th century continued to be employed in more rural areas, away from the Atlantic coast. Provided with old-fashioned leaded casement windows and high, gabled roofs, and often of asymmetrical design, these simple homes were usually built of wood, sometimes hung with tiles or shingles. In New England these Colonial homes, with their steeply pitched roofs and two-storeyed construction (the upper storey 'jettied' or projected beyond the lower storey), were instantly recognizable by their large central chimneys, which helped to warm the rooms on either side on every floor. In Pennsylvania the influence of German and Dutch settlers could clearly be seen in the flared, unduly prominent hipped roofs and thick wood or even stone walls. Houses further south were, as a rule, lower – often of just one storey – and provided with chimney stacks at both gabled ends of the pitched roof. In contrast to the more complex plans of their northeastern cousins, Colonial homes in the south were designed with only a central passageway, sited, as a commentator of 1724 explained, 'through the middle of the house for an air-draught in summer'.

By 1740, however, metropolitan areas on the east coast – particularly the cities of Boston, Philadelphia, Charleston and Alexandria (whose grid of streets was laid out in 1748 by George Washington, among others) – were beginning to import the new,

ABOVE: *Striking yellow ochre paint complements this typically Early Palladian interior of the dining room at Gunston Hall, Virginia, designed and carved by William Buckland after 1755.*

OPPOSITE: *Mid-18th-century brick townhouse, with especially prominent dormer windows, in the heart of Philadelphia's Society Hill. The district was first laid out in 1681 by the London-based Free Society of Traders; however, most of the area was developed after 1740.*

35

The handsome, Palladian-proportioned brick elevation of the Hammond-Harwood House in Annapolis, Maryland, has been termed the finest Colonial facade in America. Built in 1774–6 for plantation owner Mathias Hammond, the house was designed by British émigré William Buckland, a joiner who blossomed as an architect once he crossed the Atlantic.

Palladian fashion from Britain to create the first true 'Georgian' houses in America. With their symmetrical facades, sash windows and external shutters, these regularly proportioned homes were a marked improvement on the traditional Colonial house. For the first time brick, rather than wood, became the preferred material for facing individual elevations, which began to be grouped in terraces in the manner of London and Bath. (Philadelphia's Society Hill, a brick-built development of great sophistication begun in 1750, was one of the first of these developments.) And, in sharp contrast to their predecessors, these new Palladian house types were unusually spacious, being at least two rooms deep. (As Marcus Whiffen noted, 'no 17th century house in the English colonies was more than one room deep under the main roof, though added back rooms were often accommodated under a lean-to or shed roof.')

Away from the new urban terraces, grander Palladian homes were by 1750 being provided with Venetian windows (termed 'Palladian windows' in America), pilasters and, for the first time, small Classical porticoes to emphasize the entrance. Yet these homes were by no means carbon copies of the Palladian villas or terraced houses being erected in Britain at this time. American builders and designers remained particularly fond of the steeply pitched roof with dormers, a feature which had been common in Dutch and British designs of the late 17th century and which was especially beloved of Dutch immigrants. The peculiarly American synthesis of English Palladian and Pre-Georgian Dutch provided a template for upper-middle-class dwellings which was to endure well into the 19th century.

The spread of Palladian ideas and Georgian proportions along the east coast and even into the interior was greatly aided by the profusion of printed design sources from Britain. By the middle of the 18th century, British pattern-books were being used as sources for structural and decorative features; elements culled from works such as James Gibbs' *Book of Architecture* of 1728 and William Salmon's *Palladio Londinensis* of 1734 appeared regularly on the inside as well as the outside of American homes of all shapes and sizes. Indeed, the characteristic 'Gibbs surround' of a rusticated architrave framing a door or window, which appeared in Gibbs' 1728 volume, became even more popular in Colonial America than it was in Georgian Britain.

For much of the 18th century, Americans relied heavily not only on British pattern-books and materials, but also on emigrant British designers. In 1751, for example, the architect John Ariss arrived in Maryland from England, and promptly placed an advertisement in the local paper extolling his ability to design 'Buildings of all Sorts and Dimensions . . . either of the Ancient or Modern Order of Gibbs' Architect'. In many cases, as Sir John Summerson observed, the grander Colonial homes of the first half of the century 'were designed by leading British or British-trained craftsmen who proceeded on the basis of some existing model and the owner's verbal instructions.'

British emigrants were not, of course, the only designers to exercise an influence on the American house. The simple, pragmatic utilitarianism of the Dutch, German and Scandinavian settlers of America's east coast did much to transform the average interior, in a manner that is still widely admired and much copied today. The Dutch influence in New York, for instance – which derived from the city's days as the Dutch colony of New Amsterdam – remained strong well into the 19th century. 'Dutch colonial' houses, with their steep, double-pitched or gambrel roofs (sometimes with extravagantly flared eaves) are still to be found in New York and its environs. At the same time, the French settlers in Louisiana were building houses that reminded them of their homeland or, more usually, of the type that their fellow-colonists were erecting in

The Small Dining Room at George Washington's home of Mount Vernon, Virginia, originally of the 1770s, features a fine plaster ceiling, festoon curtains and a carved chimneypiece and overmantel taken from a design in one of the British, Palladian-inspired pattern-books published earlier in the century.

the West Indies, where the climate more resembled that of the Mississippi valley. The full-length porch or *galerie* bordered by tall, floor-length windows, which became such an integral feature of the southern home, was probably borrowed from French West Indian sources.

Before the end of the Revolutionary War, the Adam brothers' highly influential style had crossed the Atlantic and gained a foothold in the new Republic. The first true example of this light, graceful and more correctly Neoclassical manner can be found in George Washington's dining room at Mount Vernon, designed in 1775. The first house built entirely in the fashion of the Adams, however, did not appear until after the Revolution. Interestingly, this house – Woodlands, in Philadelphia – was erected in 1787–9 to the design not of an established architect, but of the house's owner, William Hamilton.

While few households could afford the splendours of Mount Vernon or Woodlands, the Neoclassical language that these great houses introduced into America soon became part of the regular vocabulary of the average, middle-class dwelling. Even the most modest, post-revolutionary Federal homes began to demonstrate an awareness of both the lighter, more graceful Adam style and the newer, more archaeologically correct forms being propounded by the leading designers of the British Regency. Fanlights became more prominent, walls higher and roofs lower, creating a facade that was dominated not, as formerly, by a dormer-strewn pitched roof with prominent chimney stacks, but by the grid of symmetrically arranged sash windows with their accompanying wooden shutters.

West elevation of Thomas Jefferson's design for his own house at Monticello, Virginia. Drawn by Jefferson's pupil Robert Mills some time after 1803.

While post-revolutionary America enthusiastically embraced the Adam brothers' synthesis of Neoclassical and Palladian influences, using this as the basis for the new Federal style, the growing self-confidence of the new Republic, allied to the constant stream of immigrants arriving in her cities, meant that by 1800 American domestic architecture exhibited a diversity that had not been seen before. Individual communities combined local materials with their own cultural heritage to produce robust homes of great charm which were not reproduced in any other region. When, for example, work began on the Shakers' new settlement of Shakertown in Kentucky (which became the last Shaker community to disband, in 1922), the Shakers looked not to the latest Regency or Greek Revival forms but to the simpler design of early 18th-century Colonial homes, fusing early 18th-century facades with interiors that were starkly bare and minimalist in a distinctly Scandinavian manner. In the south, coastal cities such as Charleston and Wilmington took the Caribbean concept of the balconied house even further, resulting in long, narrow, multistoreyed, wooden-framed houses with porches, designed to catch the sea breezes, along the whole length of each floor. (Wilmington's Burgwin-Wright house of 1770 actually has two sets of balconies on each side of a three-storeyed, weatherboarded composition.)

Adam style: the dining room at Monticello, Virginia (completed in 1809), showing a delicate chimneypiece and shield-back chairs reinterpreted in the simpler language of American Federalism.

Further north, architects and builders experimented more with brick and, if it was available, stone construction, and were not averse to borrowing from Britain when they wished to create a metropolitan home of considerable sophistication. In the northeast, two of America's most influential early architects, Boston-based Charles Bulfinch and Salem-based Samuel McIntire, began to incorporate Regency motifs into their works, the austerity and understatement of much Regency design greatly appealing to the New England temperament. Bulfinch's Harrison Gray Otis House in Boston (1796) neatly typifies the stylistic synthesis adopted by the architects and builders of the time: on the exterior traditional Palladian motifs – the Venetian and lunette windows – are combined with a most Adamesque front door, complete with a broad yet delicate fanlight; inside, the restrained mouldings and bright colours are of the latest Regency style.

By 1800, America was able to boast a wide range of home-grown architectural talent. The first great native-born American architect was, of course, none other than the Third President of the United States, Thomas Jefferson. Jefferson's practice was, even more than those of contemporary rivals such as Bulfinch, largely limited to grand projects – in his case, to Virginia villas and to the new works at the University of Virginia. However, Jeffersonian Classicism also profoundly influenced the way the average home developed, bequeathing to posterity one of the most characteristic elements of the 19th-century American home, the Greek portico. By the time of Jefferson's death in 1826, Grecian porticoes were being applied not just to grand country mansions, but to all manner of humble urban and rural homes, whether of brick, stone or merely wood. Indeed, a house was not considered properly dressed (nor of sufficient social pretension) without one.

Even during Jefferson's day, however, while Federal elevations departed ever further from British models, America remained unduly dependent on Britain for the elements used to furnish or decorate the interior of the average home. The British stranglehold on decorative items had been very strong before 1776; few French textiles, for example, made it across the Atlantic. Yet, while the Treaty of Paris in 1783, and especially

Delicate, Adamesque decoration, Hepplewhite shield-back chairs, Regency-style 'French rod' curtains and a fine reproduction carpet show how much British design still influenced Federal America at the turn of the 19th century. This corridor is from the Gardner-Pingree House in Salem, Massachusetts, built in 1805 to the designs of Samuel McIntire for a wealthy local merchant.

Napoleon's blockade of Britain in 1810, inevitably opened up possibilities of new foreign trade, it took the new Republic until the middle of the 19th century to properly rid itself of pre-revolutionary trading arrangements and decorative habits. After 1783 French wallpapers – generally featuring floral, architectural or landscape designs – suddenly flooded onto the market; by the 1790s, too, the new United States was trading directly with the Far East for luxury goods such as porcelain and floor matting. Yet most items for furnishing the house still came from Britain.

One of the principal reasons for the delay in establishing American production was that new industrial technology remained a closely guarded secret in Britain – even more so, of course, after the formal severance of the colonies in 1783. As Jane Nylander has pointed out: 'Not until after 1825 did American textile manufacturers begin to provide any serious competition for imported goods.' As a result, even a grand, post-revolutionary house such as Homewood in Baltimore – a home completely remodelled in the latest Regency style between 1798 and 1801 – was still entirely furnished with imported, British fittings.

The importation of floor coverings is a typical example of this dependency. In 1776 Philadelphia was the largest city in the newly proclaimed United States; yet, as Rosenstiel and Winkler have noted, in this city 'floor coverings of any type appeared in less than three per cent of the inventories that have survived'. Indeed, throughout the 18th century most Americans were still using oriental carpets as table-covers (although in 1766 Benjamin Franklin celebrated the repeal of the notorious Stamp Act by purchasing a Turkey carpet costing the sizeable sum of ten guineas). By 1787 American Axminsters were being made for the first time – in Philadelphia, by William Sprague, who had worked at the original Axminster factory but had emigrated to New Jersey after the Revolution. In 1791 Sprague's Philadelphia factory was weaving carpets for the Senate Chamber and for President Washington's lodgings; at the same time the firm was supplying humble ingrain carpets to all manner of households. Yet in 1830 most superior pile carpets – Axminsters, Wiltons and Brussels – still came from Britain, rather than from American factories; it was only in the 1840s that American carpet production (centred by this time both on Philadelphia and on the larger Connecticut towns) actually overtook the level of British imports. Floorcloths, too, were still being imported from Britain until well after the Revolution. Long popular in America (as early as 1700 they were used by such dignitaries as the Govenors of Massachusetts and Virginia), by the end of the century the simpler versions were finally being made in the US (in 1796, George Washington purchased a floorcloth, costing $14.28, for use at Mount Vernon). However, it was not until the early decades of the 19th century that the American floorcloth industry truly began to flourish.

The same remains true of many of the other decorative products destined for the middle-class home. Chandeliers, together with all but the most basic candlesticks, were imported into America from Britain until long after the Revolution, since American brass foundries and glassworks were not properly developed until the early 19th century. Some decorative ironwork, it was true, could be made locally before 1800. A panorama of Charleston, South Carolina, drawn in 1739, for example, shows almost every house equipped with one or even two decorated balconies – some of them made of wood, but many of iron. Yet by 1776 complex large scale pieces (in Charleston's case, an iron altar rail for the church) were still being ordered from Britain. It took the Declaration of Independence to make this a far less attractive option, and to provide the necessary spur for the native iron masters to develop their own skills. By 1830 there were few who were not fully aware of the very latest developments in the iron industry, and indeed of all of the new technologies that were revolutionizing how the average home was designed, built and used.

Georgian innovation translated to America: splendid, cream-painted sixteen-over-sixteen pane sash windows in the kitchen dependency at Stratford, Virginia, which dates from the late 1730s. America was one of the few places enthusiastically to adopt the British invention of the double-hung sash window.

Using the Georgian House

T HE BASIC PLAN of the Georgian home was much the same for First Rate as for Fourth Rate houses. In 1772 Pierre-Jean Grosley observed that 'a subterraneous storey, occupied by kitchen and offices', was a common feature in most terrace houses. This basement did not need to function as a store for coal: since the 1720s coal had – at least in the larger towns and cities – been stored in specially built vaults which ran under the street itself. In 1756 Isaac Ware noted that 'the basement is naturally the kitchen', although it could additionally serve as accommodation for the servants if the garrets proved too small, in which case 'a bed for a man or 2 maid servants is contrived to be let down in the kitchen.'

The drawing room (or the more humble parlour) was often placed on the ground floor, so as to be near the main entrance, while the dining room was often moved down a floor from its accustomed place on the Palladian *piano nobile*, so as to be both nearer the kitchen and to provide an easy progression for guests who were being entertained in the drawing room prior to eating.

As the 18th century progressed, the parlour and the drawing room, at least in the grander middle-class homes, began to take on differing roles. While the parlour became more and more a private room for the family to retire to, the drawing room (in households which could afford such an addition) increasingly became the focus of the fashionable Georgian house. The drawing room had begun life in the 16th century as a private 'withdrawing' chamber to repair to after a busy social event. In the 17th century it became larger, and more accessible to visitors, and by the mid-18th century was well established as the principal reception room of the house, where guests were received and where, as Congreve observed, women 'retired to their tea and scandal after dinner'. Both of these functions – as a place to greet visitors, and as a refuge for the women of the house – exercised an important influence on the character of the drawing room. All of the best fittings, furnishings and coverings were installed here.

ABOVE: *An impressive half-landing, decorated with inlay, of a mid-18th-century oak staircase at Salisbury, Wiltshire*

OPPOSITE: *A Spitalfields drawing room of the 1720s, with the original window shutters in constant use. Using existing shutters can often not only obviate the need for curtains (which were, in fact, quite rare during the first half of the 18th century), but also help to keep the room warm, making the provision of double or secondary glazing quite unnecessary.*

43

And these were often decorated in what was acknowledged to be an essentially 'feminine' style as opposed, say, to the traditional, gloomy masculinity of the dining room. As such the drawing room was comparatively light and airy, with an emphasis on brightly coloured wall and floor finishes and, of course, on comfort.

Not only was the drawing room more brightly decorated than the other rooms of the house; it was also better lit. As glass technology advanced, and it became possible to make larger areas of glass, drawing room windows became ever longer and wider. By the early 19th century they were often extended right down to the floor, and some were permanently propped open in order to allow guests access onto the newly fashionable, green-painted iron verandahs. At the other end of the room, mahogany double doors, which helped give an impression of greater space and light, as well as grandeur and drama, were by 1800 a common feature.

These double doors could lead into the dining room; alternatively, the dining room could, in accordance with the traditional practice of Italian villa architecture, be left on the first floor, and a more private parlour be inserted on the ground floor. However, the further away from the ground floor or basement kitchen the dining room was, then clearly the colder food would get on its journey to the table. When it did arrive, it was eaten in an atmosphere that was deliberately kept dark and austere – plain reds and greens being favoured by the end of the 18th century for decorating the walls and upholstering the seat furniture.

If the first floor no longer held both the drawing and dining rooms, it often, at least in the grander houses, featured a large room for entertaining on a grand scale. This room, designed to function along the lines of the French salon (and thus often termed the 'saloon'), could accommodate dancing, card-playing, or any other of the fashionable pastimes of the Georgian middle classes.

The first floor also generally accommodated the principal bedrooms, whose dimensions, as Ware noted, were 'laid out in just proportion to the extent of the ground [floor] plan'. Ware in 1756, and La Rochefoucauld in 1784, testified to the presence of the bedrooms at this level, the Frenchman adding that (in contrast to modern practice) bedrooms were generally placed at the front of the house. Other, less important bedrooms – the children's, perhaps, or the lodger's – would be placed on the plainer and meaner second floor, while the attic was reserved for servants (whose beds were often let down from the attic walls). Bedrooms would in general be decorated in lighter tones than the principal rooms on the ground floor, blues or yellows being recommended by the new interior decoration manuals of the early 19th century. The aim was to make these rooms light-hearted and welcoming, using the sort of fresh, bright colours which could nicely set off the predominantly white bedclothes and covers. Inevitably, though, there was a considerable difference between the type of decoration used for the householder's bedroom and that employed in a child's or a servant's bedchamber; little expense would be lavished on the latter, which would be painted in the cheapest colours available, or perhaps hung with an inexpensive, repeating paper.

As you rose up the house, of course, so the complexity of mouldings and the room decoration diminished with the dimensions and, most importantly, with the relative social significance of their location. Thus, while the drawing room on the ground or first floor may have featured elaborate cornices and rich, heavy doorcases, rooms at the top of the house possessed only simple box cornices, a rudimentary dado and perhaps

OPPOSITE: *This axonometric drawing of a typical Bath townhouse – 26 Great Pulteney Street, drawn by Richard Neville – clearly shows exactly how a townhouse of the period (in this case the late 18th century) was constructed. Note the M-shaped roof, with its vulnerable central gutter, and the contrasting flooring materials: dressed stone or marble in the entrance hall, wooden boards on the floors above and rough flags for the basement and area.*

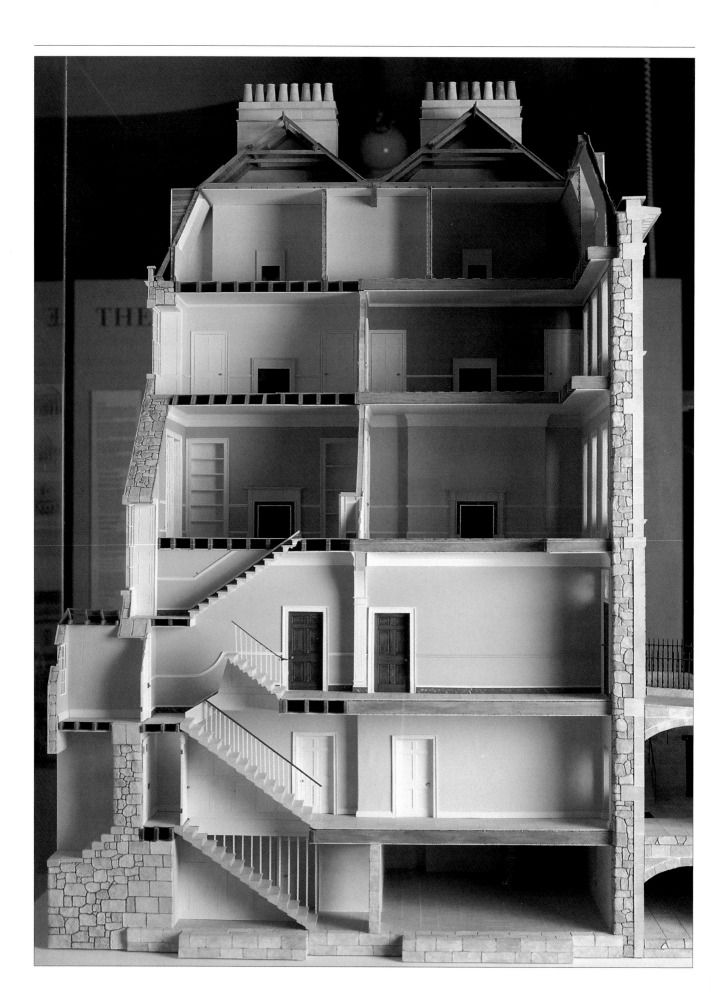

no skirting mouldings at all. Decoration was proportional to the pretensions of the room; the humbler the function – and indeed the fewer the visitors – then the more modest the mouldings and furnishings would be. Ascending beyond the first floor, the visitor would notice how the decoration was being visibly pared down, and the fixtures and fittings were becoming simpler and plainer.

In the great houses of Britain and America the kitchen was often placed in an adjoining wing or subsidiary building. In the typical Georgian terraced house, however, it was invariably sited on the ground floor or in the basement. If the house was fortunate enough to boast a large rear yard, then the kitchen, laundry and other working areas may have been relegated to a separate structure there.

By 1700 most cooking was no longer done on the floor of an open hearth in the kitchen but over a more sophisticated wrought-iron basket – the grate. As the century progressed, the workings of the grate or range became ever more complex and heat-efficient. The ancestor of the range, the 'perpetual oven' combining oven and grate, appeared *c*.1750; by the 1780s the iron boiler was being combined with the grate and the oven in a cast iron, wood- or coal-fired kitchen range. Joseph Langmead's patent range of 1783 effectively provided the basic pattern for ranges for the next two centuries. In many humble houses and cottages, of course, cooking was still done over an open hearth as late as the middle of the 20th century. J.C. Loudon was perhaps rather over-optimistic in hoping in 1833 that 'the day is not very far distant when open fireplaces will be considered as relics of barbarism.'

Although the Early Georgian kitchen grate was fairly crude by modern standards, around it were installed a wide variety of technological aids quite surprising in their sophistication. Spits were rested on hooks joined to the two front legs of the grate, and were turned by an ingenious mechanical device powered by clockwork or simply by a 'smokejack', which used the force of the updraught up the kitchen chimney. Pan

LEFT: *The kitchen from a Bristol townhouse, now known as The Georgian House, in Great George Street. The house was built in 1788–91 for sugar merchant John Pinney, and while some of the utensils seen here are more recent additions, many of the items – together with the chimney surround, spit and oven – are as found in Pinney's kitchen.*

OPPOSITE: *A model by Lionel Currie of 26 Great Pulteney Street, Bath. The street was laid out by Thomas Baldwin in the late 1780s; however, the disposition and decoration of each interior would have been decided by the first owner.*

supports ('trivets'), also attached to the grate, could swing out over the fire; later this arrangement metamorphosed into the hob grate. The 1710 Inventory of the Great and Little Kitchens at Dyrham Park, Gloucestershire, included an impressive array of kitchen technology: an 'Iron Crane', iron racks, '5 Spitts', '2 Dripping panns', four brass kettles, brass pots, '2 Bell metall Skillets', and a bewildering variety of other brass, iron and pewter kitchenware.

The food cooked in the Georgian kitchen is becoming increasingly familiar to today's more historically conscious enthusiasts. Gradually the legacy of the medieval and Tudor periods, which saw much intermingling of what we would now regard as sweet and savoury tastes, was diluted by more fashionably French and, to our minds, more visibly 20th-century fare.

The Dyrham Park inventory of 1710 tells us much about the eating habits of the wealthier households at the beginning of the Georgian era. The kitchen contained a bacon rack, two salt boxes, '4 pye plates', plates for cheese and for fish, a 'Beef Fork' and an oatmeal mill; particularly indicative of the comparative wealth of the house-owner was a 'Tin Chocolate pot' and three copper coffee pots.

During the 18th century main dishes were primarily roasted, boiled or stewed, or baked in the nearby oven or stove. For the higher echelons of Georgian society, the

The smokehouse at Mount Vernon, set well away from the house to keep cooking and curing smells out of the principal rooms.

*Typical 18th-century
cooking and eating
implements from the
Crowninshield-Bentley
House, part of the Essex
Institute Museum site in
Salem, Massachusetts.*

principal emphasis for main meals was on meat dishes and, to a lesser extent, on fish; the lower-middle classes, however, had to make do with cabbages (and their numerous relatives), pulses, beans, root vegetables, oatmeal, barley, bread and bacon. By the mid-18th century heavy suet puddings – which had replaced the medieval cereal porages – had become common. Yet it was only by the end of the 18th century that raw fruit was widely accepted as being safe to eat. Fruit consumption received a great boost from the introduction of the heated greenhouse in which vines and peach, fig, lemon and orange trees could all be easily grown, and by 1830 fruit-growing had become remarkably prevalent.

As Georgian eating habits developed, so did mealtimes. Modern-style breakfasts – very much a Georgian invention – were by the middle of the 18th century taken at 9 or 10 in the morning. This development in turn caused dinner, the main meal of the day, to be put back from noon to 2 or even 3 o'clock. By the end of the century the most fashionable urban households were eating their dinner at 4 or 5, necessitating the creation of two new meals: a later 'supper' of cold collations, taken at about 10pm, and a midday 'luncheon' to bridge the ever-widening gap between breakfast and dinner. While such arrangements found enthusiastic adherents in London and the major metropolitan centres, however, many provincial (and colonial) households preferred to stick with the mealtimes – and the meal names – they were used to. As a result, 'dinner' is still the name for the midday meal in many parts of Britain and America.

49

*The laundry at 7 Great
George Street, Bristol,
complete with plate rack
and an original,
18th-century box mangle.*

A rare, stone-lined cold-water plunge bath of c.1790, from Bristol's Georgian House museum. Georgian domestic baths rarely survive today; most bathrooms in Georgian houses have subsequently been redeveloped. It must be admitted, also, that most Georgians were decidedly averse to bathing. The owner of this house, however, was rather keener on keeping clean than most of his contemporaries. As a youth John Pinney had boasted that 'I now subscribe to a Cold Bath and goes in every morning which I finds to be of great service to me' – a habit he clearly maintained throughout his adulthood.

In contrast to the relative sophistication of the kitchen, the Georgian bathroom was generally a very basic facility. Simple plunge baths – filled not by taps but by water brought from the kitchen – were introduced into more hygiene-conscious middle-class homes during the second half of the 18th century. Britons, however, were notoriously slow at encompassing the latest trends in washing. It was only during the last decades of the 19th century that the average home began to be equipped with a bathroom that boasted a water closet (first patented in 1775, and generally available from 1787) and a wooden or metal bath as well as the ubiquitous freestanding washstand or dresser. For the very avant-garde, though, rudimentary showers were on the market by 1820.

Surprisingly, few of these bathrooms would have been supplied with piped water. At the beginning of the Georgian period those who did enjoy mains water had it supplied to the house – usually just to the kitchen – in wooden pipes. By the end of the 18th century new steam pumps, which increased the levels of water pressure, swiftly revealed the inadequacies of the pipe jointing, and serious ruptures were common. An important step forward was made in 1817, however, when the Metropolitan Paving Act stipulated that all water companies were in future to lay cast iron, not wooden, pipes.

Hot water for the later Georgian house was generally brought up from the kitchen, where it was heated in a rectangular boiler. This often extended round the back of the fire for more economical heating, and was filled through a lid on the top and emptied via a tap on the side. Lead cisterns to hold the water needed for kitchen use were often now placed inside the kitchen and not, as formerly, left outside in the yard or garden. Increasingly they were supplemented by sinks, often placed behind a partition to create a scullery area quite separate from the space in which food was prepared. Earlier Georgian sinks were generally made of stone or wood, and lined with lead – although Neil Burton has pointed out that some were actually hewn from a single piece of stone. By 1800, however, ceramic examples were becoming widely available, and by 1830 a number of catalogues were featuring off-the-peg kitchenware of this type.

Most Late Georgian or Federal householders could not afford to pay the water companies for a 'high service' (water pumped to the upper floors). Instead, they settled for

A surviving, late-18th-century brick drain from Mount Vernon, Virginia.

53

View from the laundry window at 7 Great George Street, Bristol, showing the original stone sink and handpump which supplied rainwater to the kitchen and laundry. Rainwater – collected from the roof, and stored in a sealed tank under the laundry – was the only source of water for this Late Georgian, middle-class townhouse.

the cheaper option of a ground floor mains supply only, and carried water upstairs by hand. The effect of this 'low service' was to inconvenience the inhabitants of the upper floors; in an age where many homes were in multiple occupancy (often with a different family or lodger on each floor), this further dramatized the social stratifications of the house. As Grose observed in 1795, the dignity of each class of resident in the house was 'in the inverse ratio of altitude'. Servants and upstairs lodgers, faced with the arduous descent to the kitchen for their water, were constantly reminded of their lowly social status. It was certainly no fun to be poor in the Georgian period.

The Mount Vernon washhouse.

THE DETAILS

6

Brickwork

B RICKS WERE FIRST brought to Britain by the Romans (and to America by the British and Dutch). Only during the 16th century, however, did bricks become widely used in Britain, and it was not until the late 17th century that the elaborate brick structures and forms of continental Europe began to be widely mimicked. These more ambitious brick buildings were sited in the southern and eastern parts of the country, where the materials used to make bricks were easily found and where the influence of the Dutch – masters of brick building – was more strongly felt.

The restoration of King Charles II in 1660 marked the beginning of the golden age of brick building in Britain and America. Precisely moulded – and therefore highly expensive – 'gauged' or 'rubbed' bricks began to be imported on a large scale from Holland, whose buildings continued to provide the inspiration for countless British architects and craftsmen. The brick boom was given further impetus by the Great Fire of London in 1666, following which the capital's authorities made strenuous efforts to ensure that all new masonry was constructed largely from brick or stone, and was not unduly reliant on inflammable timber. The provincial towns and cities of Britain and America were quick to follow suit, and by 1720 brick-walled houses were the rule from Newcastle to Philadelphia.

During the 18th century both technology and fashion did much to alter the colour of bricks. The same basic materials – local clay and sand – continued to be used in manufacture; however, more sophisticated kilns began to appear alongside the more primitive, traditional methods of firing bricks – the rudimentary, temporary clamps and the permanent, brick-walled clamps (also called 'scotch kilns'). These new kilns abandoned the tried and trusted fuels such as wood, charcoal, bracken or heather in favour of the driving force of the Industrial Revolution: coal. Coal-fired kilns could provide a far greater range of brick colours than was possible before, the increased heat produced by the coal prompting new chemical reactions in the clay-and-sand mix.

ABOVE: *Grey, vitrified headers contrasting with red brick window dressings in a Sussex facade.*

OPPOSITE: *Vitrified headers used with red place bricks to create a checkerboard effect in Philadelphia's Society Hill.*

59

Brick-drying sheds in Hampshire. Here the raw bricks are dried before firing in the kilns.

Greater heat efficiency also aided the manufacture of the ever-popular, blue-grey 'vitri-fied' bricks – bricks placed so close to the kiln's fire-holes that the intense heat reacted with the lime in the clay to produce a silvery, glazed effect on the brick's surface. Since vitrified bricks were now more easily made, they were consequently cheaper, too; thus builders could use them not just in combination with red bricks, to form the familiar diaper or chessboard patterns, but also to form whole facades on their own.

By the mid-18th century paler brick colours were becoming more fashionable. White, yellow or grey bricks could be used to suggest (although hardly to mimic) expensive stonework; in contrast, the traditional red brick only served to remind houseowners of the humble and outmoded brick dwellings of the past. As a result, red place bricks were often relegated to a distinctly secondary role, and used only for window or door dress-ings. If a white or cream brick was still not deemed pale enough after firing, then a more convincing 'stone colour' could be obtained by limewashing the brick to give it a whiter sheen. Alternatively, additives could be introduced into the actual mix to ensure a satisfactory colour. 'Marls', for example, were white or yellow bricks whose colour was largely determined by the addition of chalk to the clay and sand.

In September 1784 a brick tax of 2s. 6d. per thousand was imposed on all British bricks, in order to help pay for the recently concluded American war. However, nei-ther this measure, nor the subsequent tax increases of 1794 and 1803, nor even the periodic slumps in the brick trade due to the French wars of 1793–1815, caused irreparable harm to the health of the brickmaking industry. Indeed the years following the Treaty of Vienna of 1815 witnessed a great building boom, which in turn helped fuel a remarkable period of growth in the brick trade. This was given further assistance by the appearance in the 1830s of brickmaking machines, able to press out individual raw bricks or even to produce a continuous raw brick shape using a mechanical extru-sion process.

The 1784 brick tax is often cited as the catalyst which promoted the use of mathematical tiles – ceramic tiles, made in the same way as bricks, and provided with large pegs at the rear which, when the tiles were nailed in overlapping layers on a vertical wall, resembled brick courses. However, mathematical tiles had been in use in southeast England since the 17th century (and were, anyway, also covered by the 1784 tax). Manufactured in as many colours as their brick cousins, they were bedded into mortar or fixed by nails onto wooden boards, which were themselves anchored onto the wall or frame behind. Inevitably, though, the surface of the completed tiling was never as uniformly flat as that of a brick wall (although perhaps even more attractive), while tiling round corners proved impossible – necessitating the provision of painted wooden boards at the end of each elevation. Nevertheless, by the end of the 18th century mathematical tiles were becoming particularly popular in the fashionable seaside towns of Kent and Sussex; indeed, they are still in widespread use – and manufactured – in these areas today.

Black, glazed mathematical tiles at Brighton's Royal Crescent (1798–1807).

Mathematical tiles in a frame, showing how they are fixed by nails onto wooden boards.

61

British brick sizes varied widely until 1840, when a standardized product – the 'Imperial' brick, measuring 9 in x 4½ in x 3 in – was formally introduced. This was only superseded in Britain in 1970, by the slightly larger metric brick (225 mm x 112.5 mm x 75 mm).

BRICK TERMS

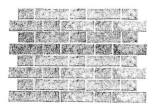

FLEMISH BOND

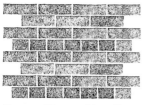

ENGLISH GARDEN WALL BOND

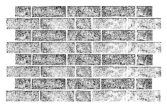

FLEMISH GARDEN WALL BOND

HEADER BOND

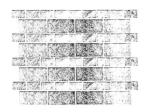

DEARNE'S BOND

Five different types of bonding.

Frog The large, V-shaped indentation in the top of a brick. Designed to save weight and to provide a key for the mortar.

Header The short face of a brick.

Stretcher The long face of a brick.

Arris A brick edge or corner.

Closer A brick cut to half a header, used to terminate the course. A **queen closer** is a brick that has been cut longitudinally; a **king closer** has one corner lopped off obliquely.

Stock brick The 'stock board' was originally the base in which wholly hand-made bricks were moulded. By 1780, however, a 'stock brick' had come to mean any brick of average shape and strength which could be used for visible work which needed reasonable quality products (also referred to as a **common** or **facing** brick).

Place brick An inferior quality, underburnt brick, used for hidden elements such as inner walls.

Clinker An overburnt and misshapen brick. Clinkers were used on occasion by unscrupulous builders for unseen walls, but more often were relegated to the garden.

Rubbed or gauged brick A soft, precisely measured brick that can be easily cut or rubbed to the exact size required. Such bricks were expensive to make, and were accordingly used sparingly – often only for brick arches. Clearly, very little mortar is needed in pointing these accurately designed products; the paper-thin joints of white mortar visible between them constitute an excellent demonstration of the bricklayer's art.

Bonding The pattern in which the brick courses are laid. There are many different types: Georgian brick walls were generally constructed in header, English or, most commonly, Flemish bond. After the brick tax of 1784 more economical – yet structurally weaker – bonds were devised, such as Rat Trap and Dearne's bonds. Note that English Garden Wall Bond is known as American Bond in the US.

Pointing The protective mortar finish to a joint between two bricks. Known as **jointing** in America.

Mortar Traditionally, the lime-based putty used for pointing. Mortar is not intended to be 'glue' for bricks – which should, if well laid, be able to hold their position as a result of gravity. It is instead designed to fill the gaps between the joints, thus preventing water from penetrating the masonry, and to help spread the weight load.

MAINTENANCE AND REPAIR

Brickwork is one of the most characteristic and attractive elements of the average Georgian home. The vast array of brick colours, textures and shapes makes an enormous contribution to the visual interest of even the most modest Georgian facade, and does much to define the character of the townscape. However, in countless instances appealing brickwork is ruined both aesthetically and structurally by misguided repairs, or simply by bad repointing.

1

2

3

4

5

6

7

REPOINTING

Repointing is a process that requires considerable skill and experience. In dealing with an old building, it is essential to employ craftsmen who are able to produce a first-rate job. Many fine buildings have been permanently spoiled by well intentioned but poorly executed amateur repointing. It is thus always helpful to ask your bricklayer to provide test samples of his work – and of the mortar he will use – before he starts on the wall itself.

Bad repointing of an old wall can not only look unsightly, but can cause serious erosion of the masonry through the action of rainwater and of the harmful soluble salts that the rain carries. The two main essentials to remember when repointing are (1) to avoid any method of repointing that encourages water to collect on, and thus ultimately penetrate, the brickwork, and (2) to avoid using cement-rich mortars.

Key to pointing terms:

1 *Flush Joint* *The most common traditional form of pointing, where the mortar is finished flush with the brick face.*

2 *Flush Scribed Joint* *Often seen in 18th-century work. The flush pointing is scribed with a rule and trowel end shortly before the mortar sets, producing a neat lined-out appearance in otherwise relatively irregular work.*

3 *Keyed Joint* *Not to be confused with the rather exaggerated modern raked joint. The mortar is pressed into the joint with a bucket handle or similar curved tool to give a slightly concave section. Useful in some cases for repointing old work where the bricks are irregular.*

4 *Tuck Pointing* *An elaborate technique used particularly in the second half of the 18th-century. Where the effect of fine*

brickwork was required from lower quality work, the joints were flush-pointed with mortar coloured to match the bricks. Before this set, a groove was cut into the mortar to receive a thin line of carefully sieved lime putty.

5 *Struck Pointing* *Commonly used in modern brickwork; the hard mortar slopes in from the bed joints to cast off the rain. This type of pointing produces a hard line and is rarely suitable for restoration purposes.*

6 *Overhand Struck Pointing* *Struck pointing with the slope reversed is sometimes used in old brickwork.*

7 *Beaked Joint* *A kind of double struck pointing more usually associated with stonework but occasionally used in brickwork where the sharp line achieved was thought desirable.*

A leaking downpipe has caused the brickwork of this Fournier Street house to erode. Subsequent repointing in cement has done little to help, hastening the decay of the bricks and resulting in the cement ultimately falling out. Repointing of old bricks must always be done in a lime-based mortar; and before any remedial work is begun, the source of the erosion – in this case the leaking downpipe – must be tackled.

Ivy can look attractive on an old building, but it can cause structural damage. Here ivy has been cleared away from the brick facade, showing where the roots have been eating into the mortar.

For most domestic repointing, mortars based on lime – burnt and slaked calcium carbonate – are always preferable to those based on cement. Lime mortars are flexible and porous, two qualities which are essential for the preservation of a brick wall. Rainwater must be allowed to evaporate through the mortar back into the air, and must not be trapped inside the fabric of the brick itself by hard cements which are impervious to water. While cement-rich mortars set harder and quicker than lime-based mixes, they can spell disaster for an old brick wall. They are in fact far too hard: cement remains unhelpfully rigid during any movement of the wall, thus causing the bricks around it to tear. Cement also encourages water and harmful salts to evaporate through the bricks themselves rather than through the mortar, with the result that the bricks deteriorate while the cement mortar around them stands proud.

Only rarely may cement be allowed into the lime-based mix; even a small proportion can adversely affect the bricks. Owing to the reactivity of lime, though, it is always best to let an expert make the mortar. (Do check, however, that your bricklayer really is using genuine lime putty.) And remember not to attempt repointing in frosty weather: the water content of wet mortar is high and freezing conditions can cause this water to expand, and the drying mortar to crack.

Some traditional mortars were 'galleted' – studded with pieces of stone, brick or flint – to give the pointing greater visual interest or simply to fill a wide joint. Other mortars were blackened after drying, in order to direct attention away from the joints to the bricks themselves. Both effects should be respected where they survive and, if you wish, can be continued; simply ensure that the finished work is consistent with what is already there. New bricks that are far brighter than their older neighbours can be soot-washed before insertion; do, though, avoid artificial colourants for either bricks or mortars, since these are liable to fade or discolour rapidly.

TUCK POINTING

Rubbed or gauged bricks were, as we have seen, widely used to produce neat, thinly jointed brickwork. Yet they remained costly to use. Far cheaper was a Georgian sham devised to make poor quality bricks look, at a distance, like superior gauged bricks: tuck pointing. By this practice, badly cut or worn stock or even place bricks were surrounded by a base mortar the same colour as the brick itself; then a white 'tucking mortar' was inserted in a thin, straight line into the middle of the darker mortar between the bricks. Unless you were close to the wall it was often difficult to tell that the masonry did not comprise expensive, accurately cut bricks.

Tuck pointing is obviously rather a cheat. However, although it is not recommended for new walls, it is of great historic value where it survives and should be carefully restored. The Society for the Protection of Ancient Buildings (SPAB) publish an excellent, step-by-step guide to repairing tuck-pointed walls (see Further Reading, page 232).

PAINTING

It is always best to leave old brickwork completely unpainted. Modern paints do not allow the brick wall to 'breathe', trapping moisture inside the bricks themselves – which, with their high salt content, are soon worn away through the reaction of water and salts. The trapped moisture will also help to force the paint off the wall, resulting in an uneven and unsightly finish that will require constant repainting.

CLEANING

Simple water washing, performed either by hand-held brushes or with gentle sprays, is by the far the best way of cleaning old brickwork. High-powered dry- or wet-sand blasting or high-pressure water lances will remove much of the brick's surface along with the dirt. Diluted hydrofluoric acid can be used for heavily soiled bricks; this is not, however, a job for the amateur, since even in solution the acid is highly corrosive. Other chemical cleaners are not recommended, since they generally contain soluble salts which will erode the bricks. Alkaline cleaners, for example, should only be used on glazed brick surfaces.

Old limewash should be removed from bricks using a clay poultice, as it will not respond even to the hardest scrubbing. Water-thinned paints can be removed with water, after softening with steam. Polyurethane paints or other commercial emulsions have to be removed using hot air paint strippers or non-alkaline chemical paint removers. In all such cases, irreparable damage can so easily be done to the old brickwork that it is wise to consult a recognized expert before beginning any major task.

Stonework

A s Alec Clifton-Taylor noted in 1962, 'All our most stylish stone buildings are largely or wholly faced in ashlar' – that is, squared and dressed stone blocks. This is particularly true of the Georgian period, a time when many humble brick buildings were faced with ashlar in order to present a grander face to the street. Many more modest, vernacular buildings were clad not in costly ashlar but in cheaper 'rubble' stonework – blocks that had not been finished to such a fine degree and which still retained a rough outer finish. 'Dressed rubble' walling comprised rubble blocks that had been neatly squared to allow for precise, thin joints; 'free rubble' walling consisted of naturally found blocks, coursed and generously pointed as regularly as possible.

The ground floors of the grandest, stone-faced houses were rusticated – a typical Palladian device by which the deeply recessed joints helped to convey a visual impression of strength and utility. This treatment was designed to contrast with the smooth surface of the ashlar-faced principal floor above. More rustic still was the technique of vermiculation, in which the stonework was tooled to imitate worm tracks. This bizarre practice was commonly used for the walls of lodges and garden buildings from the 1730s onwards.

OPPOSITE: *Heavily pointed stonework on the facade of Cliveden, a mansion in the Germantown district of Philadelphia built in 1763–7 of local stone.*

STONE TYPES

The principal forms of building stone are limestone, sandstone, granite, marble, flint and slate. Limestone, made principally from calcium carbonate, can be found in a bewildering variety of guises. Soft, white chalk is a limestone, as is grey, coarse Kentish ragstone. Yellow or white oolite, found in a wide belt from Hull to Weymouth, is also a limestone (hard, creamy-white Portland stone, honey-coloured Bath and Cotswold stones and golden Barnack stone from Northamptonshire are all part of this immediate family), as is the blue, purple or brown lias found in a narrow band stretching from

67

Sunderland in the northeast to Lyme Regis in the southwest. Georgian architects were particularly fond of two of the most renowned limestones: Bath stone and Portland stone. If John Nash could afford to use genuine Bath stone to face a terrace, he did so. (Stucco – generally painted a yellow-brown colour in imitation of real Bath stone – was only used when financially necessary.) Portland stone, much used for grand facades since the days of Inigo Jones and Christopher Wren, was particularly prized for its fine weathering qualities – a property which is still very evident today. Not only was this material used for new buildings; many owners of existing, pre-Georgian houses had the facades of their buildings encased in Portland stone.

Sandstones are based on quartz particles, mixed with other minerals and organic remains. They can range in colour from near-white to the famous dark red sandstones of the northwest.

Granite, the hardest of the common building stones, is made from crystalline minerals fused deep in the earth at very high temperatures. Grey granite buildings can look somewhat dour in dull light; it may take sunlight or rain to bring out their sparkling constituents.

Marble, at least in Britain, often denotes any stone that can be cut and polished well. Native British marbles range from the fossil-filled 'Purbeck marble' (actually a limestone) to the dark red serpentine of southwest Cornwall and the white alabaster of Staffordshire and Nottinghamshire.

Flints are extremely hard stones, made almost entirely from silica. They can be found in areas of chalky subsoil, in areas where there has been much glacial activity, and on beaches and river beds. One of the first materials to be exploited by man, flints have been used for building in Britain since before the Roman occupation, wherever they were the readiest source of cheap stone. By the Georgian period flints were often used in conjunction with brick or stone, with finely cut ashlar or well rubbed brickwork used to relieve the monotony and to dress the edges of the rougher flintwork, as well as to provide additional structural stability. The flints themselves vary in colour according to their location – some are almost black, some grey, while those found adjacent to deposits of iron ore are streaked with brown. The purest, black-faced flints are called 'floorstones' or 'builders', and are found at the lowest level of excavation; those found above these are known as 'wallstones'.

REPOINTING STONE WALLS

The repointing of stonework should always be executed with a few key guidelines in mind. First and foremost, it is a task always best performed by a trained and experienced professional. Secondly, any new mortar should match the existing work (both the stone and the joints) in terms of colour, composition and strength. Ribbon-pointing, or any other modern practice that results in over-prominent pointing with exposed ledges, should be strenuously avoided, even if it is a well-established local tradition. Ribbon-pointing not only looks unsightly, but provides a surface on which water can collect, and from which it can subsequently penetrate and erode the stone. If a wall has been constructed with no mortar at all – i.e. a dry-stone wall – then no mortar should be added when repairing it.

It is also important to remember that lime mortars are always best for traditional masonry, and that cement mortars – even those with a small proportion of cement – are usually unacceptable. The aesthetic effect that grey cement mortar has on an old wall is rarely pleasing; more importantly for the structure, cements are simply too strong for traditional masonry materials. Hair cracks can develop in the cement; moisture is

An example of bad workmanship. In pointing or repointing random stonework, it is important not to let the beauty of the stone become overshadowed by the dominance of the pointing. Joints should be as unobtrusive as possible.

absorbed through the cracks, and is then unable to evaporate out of the wall through the stone or through the impervious mortar. The end result is the decay of the wall: frosts freeze the trapped moisture and cause it to expand, which in turn cracks the stone.

Ashlar walls need very little repointing. Any mortar needs to be applied with considerable skill, so that it is bedded deep down into the joint but does not butter over the arrises of the finely cut stones on the surface. Wetting the area to be worked on before repointing helps the mortar to fasten onto the stone.

If the wall has been galleted with small pieces of flint or other stone pieces or with fragments of glass, try to ensure that this technique is reproduced in any new work. Gallets should be pressed into the mortar, facing downwards and outwards, shortly before it sets.

Details of stone repointing techniques are clearly outlined in the SPAB's excellent leaflets (see Further Reading, page 232–3).

REPAIRING STONE WALLS

Replacement stones should, like bricks, always match their surroundings in terms of colour, shape and texture. Although it may be impossible to match the stone exactly – most quarries active during the Georgian era are now defunct – your local Conservation Officer or a national organization such as English Heritage or Men of the Stones (see Sources, page 229) should be able to direct you to a roughly comparable material.

It is traditional in many areas of what was Colonial America to build brick walls upon footings of randomly coursed stone. In this example, from Annapolis in Maryland, the pointing has been galleted with small stones – a decorative device used on both sides of the Atlantic during the Georgian period.

Serious wind erosion (above left) or delamination (above) of even good-quality stonework needs to be halted as early as possible, otherwise serious structural damage can arise.

Modern sealants are never a good idea for old stonework: they not only weather extremely badly, trapping dirt and other pollutants, but they may also erode the stonework by trapping moisture within the masonry.

One potential problem in maintaining a stone wall is the Georgians' preference for strengthening stonework by inserting iron cramps into the masonry. If moisture penetrates into the stonework the cramps inevitably rust, expanding in size and breaking up the surrounding material.

In addition, old stone or flint walls often have no damp courses within them, and are thus susceptible to rising damp. In many cases, however, the solution does not have to be as dramatic as some may think. The SPAB's publications (listed in Further Reading, page 232–3) can give detailed advice regarding sympathetic and cheap remedies for this problem.

CLEANING STONEWORK

The basic question to ask before cleaning stone is, is it really necessary? Often you will remove the attractive patina of age only to leave yourself with a patchily streaked and oddly coloured surface.

If it *is* truly necessary to clean a stone-faced terrace, at least try to ensure that the whole of the terrace is cleaned at the same time: piecemeal cleaning of uniform compositions can have distinctly jarring visual results. And make sure that the cleaning specification is precise and detailed: over-enthusiastic cleaning can easily do more harm than good. Acid cleaners can attack some types of stone; even water, when used in excessive quantities, can erode the surface of the stone and expose the vulnerable core underneath. Saturating the stone with water can also cause damp problems in the longer term, while creating areas which are easily re-soiled. Gentle, intermittent water sprays are nearly always the best answer, though poulticing or carefully controlled chemical cleaners may be required for deeper staining or stubborn paint.

Whatever method you chose, before beginning have a look at the SPAB's inexpensive guide on this subject: *Cleaning Stone and Brick.*

71

Disastrous, piecemeal repointing of this flint wall in cement mortars has caused structural failure and moisture penetration as well as the virtual obliteration of the flint faces.

REPAIRING FLINT WALLS

The repair of flint walling or flint masonry is often more difficult than it seems. Flints are not regularly shaped, like ashlar or bricks, and thus need careful treatment. Flint walls are easily ruined by bad pointing, which is not only visually unsightly, but can also cause structural damage, considerably shortening the lifespan of the masonry. When repairing or repointing flintwork it is vital to ensure both that the mortar mix is correct (see page 69), and that the placing of the stones, and the resulting relationship of flint faces to the area of mortar, is visually harmonious.

Most flints are 'knapped', i.e. riven by highly skilled knappers to produce two flat faces (the term comes from the old German verb *knapen,* to snap). This, too, is more difficult than it looks. An experienced knapper can judge exactly where to deliver the blow in order to produce two squared faces, and without damaging the stone unduly; he or she can also tell from the sound the flint makes when struck if it is flawed inside. (Flints found near the ground's surface, for example, often contain Ice Age frost-fractures, and are less suitable for knapping.) It is thus always best to leave this task to skilled operators, to avoid ending up with a pile of useless shards. If you do decide to tackle knapping yourself, ensure that you are wearing goggles to protect yourself from flying splinters.

Details of flint repointing can be found in Adela Wright's *Craft Techniques for Traditional Buildings* (Batsford, 1991). The same basic procedures can also be followed when repointing a pebble wall, of the kind found in coastal areas of the southeast and East Anglia. Remember that the shallower the flints or pebbles are bedded, the weaker the wall will be.

8

Render and Stucco

THE WHOLE FAMILY of external renders – stuccoes, mastics, Roman cements, 'Portland' cements – is a subject about which there are many misconceptions. The term 'render' generally means a durable plaster, applied over a partly rigid base, which is designed to fulfil three primary functions: to protect the wall from the weather, to provide the building with a decorative covering, and possibly to hide coarsely executed masonry.

Render – often little more than a simple combination of lime (calcium carbonate, i.e. burnt limestone) and sand – has been used to cover masonry since the days of wattle-and-daub huts. 'Stucco', a thin render, was used in Britain and America from the 18th century onwards to disguise inferior masonry as finely dressed blocks of ashlar. Although the technique of stuccoing was originated by the Romans, it was, like so many other ancient practices, rediscovered by the Italians of the Renaissance, who devised the term 'stucco' to denote a mix of powdered marble and lime. By the mid-18th century, however, 'stucco' was being used in Britain and America to mean any type of internal or external plasterwork. It was only in the early 19th century that 'stucco' came specifically to signify exterior rendering, executed to suggest fine stonework.

Stucco was first popularized in Britain by the Early Palladian architects of the 1720s. By the mid-18th century it was also being adopted by the most fashionable of America's colonial households, although the predilection for good, honest brickwork often tended to win over the whim of fashion.

Early stuccoes were sadly unreliable. In 1765 the Reverend David Wark patented what can be called the first true modern stucco. This was quickly taken up by Robert Adam and his brothers, who acquired Wark's patent in 1768; six years later the Adams seized upon an allegedly more reliable product in the form of Liardet's stucco, patented in 1773. However, both Wark's and Liardet's stuccoes (or 'mastics') were oil-based, not water-based, as is commonly the practice today. The recipe often included an

OPPOSITE: *Detail of the stuccoed centrepiece, with typical Regency detailing, in London's Mecklenburgh Square.*

75

element of lead or lead-based compounds, and boiled linseed oil which, it was widely believed, would help protect the brickwork beneath. Unfortunately, in practice the oil-based render actually trapped moisture in the brickwork, thus promoting the decay of the bricks and a corresponding deterioration of the stucco itself.

Liardet's product was first used by the Adams at 11 St James's Square, London (1774–6), and subsequently on all manner of Adam facades in and around the capital. Yet by the later 1780s the failings of this new wonder material were obvious to all, as Liardet's stucco was falling off houses all over London.

The failure of Liardet's recipe allowed for the promotion of more sophisticated rivals – most notably the Reverend James Parker's 'Parker's Roman Cement', a water-based stucco patented in 1796 and enthusiastically taken up by the terrace-builder *par excellence*, John Nash. 'Roman Cements' actually bore little relation to modern cements, but were in fact quick-setting renders based on hydraulic lime, made from limestone with a high clay content. This mixture, when combined with water or reactive materials such as pulverized fuel ash, produced a quick-setting and cheap stucco. Like their oil-based predecessors, however, these water-based stuccoes – the direct ancestors of modern stucco – were still prone to failure. Unsurprisingly, their manufacture has long since ceased, and they are difficult (though not impossible) to replicate.

A harder render, a mechanical combination of limestone and clay, now known as 'artificial cement' was first successfully manufactured in Britain in 1811. In 1824 the Leeds bricklayer Joseph Aspdin patented his 'Portland Cement', so called because of the alleged similarity of the finished artificial cement to fine, pale Portland stone. While by no means identical to tough modern 'Portland cements' (the reliability of Aspdin's product was actually rather poor), these early cements were soon extremely popular, and were by 1840 widely used in place of Georgian stuccoes.

ROUGHCAST

Many local variants of 'roughcast' – a render which was combined with graded stones and other aggregates, which were literally thrown onto the wet render – were used during the Georgian era. The resulting rough finish provided the building with a large drying surface, which was an extremely valuable asset in areas where the walls were subjected to large quantities of rainwater. As a result, roughcast became widespread in Scotland, the north of England and on the northeast coast of America – areas which saw more than their fair share of storms and bad weather. Aggregates varied according to what was locally available; the name itself also changed from area to area: 'harling' in Scotland, 'wet dash' in northwest England and 'parging' or 'dashing' in America.

'Pebbledash' was in origin a more cultivated form of roughcast, using pebbles and crushed stones to create a more harmonious finish than was possible with harling. Unfortunately, the technique of pebbledashing has today become intimately associated not with traditional lime renders but with the cement render coats indiscriminately applied to old brick walls in the hope of providing shelter from the elements. All these tough but bland finishes actually achieve is to trap moisture within the hidden brickwork behind, thus hastening the decay of the wall itself. The same can be said of the various textured cement render coatings (such as the unfortunately ubiquitous 'Tyrolean render') now available.

Pargeting on a Georgian house in Essex.

PARGETING

Panels of external rendering decorated with incised, pressed or moulded motifs – a technique known as 'pargeting' – first became common in southeast England during the reign of Henry VIII. Although particularly associated with the buildings of the 17th century, pargeting remained popular throughout the Georgian period, especially in East Anglia. During the 18th century, sophisticated timber moulds were used to impress designs on the drying render; by 1840 such moulds were being used in conjunction with increasingly harder, cement-based mixes, in order to give a crisper finish.

77

COADE STONE

Coade stone keystones in London's Bedford Square (above) and Saffron Walden, Essex (below). The latter is signed and dated 1794 on the soffit.

By the mid-1770s a material called 'Coade stone' was widely used in place of stucco for external decorative details such as keystones, plaques and quoins, for statuary and for monuments. Coade stone quickly proved far more reliable than stucco and far cheaper and more malleable than stone. The reason for this was that it was not a render but a durable ceramic, made by Eleanor Coade at the Artificial Stone Manufactory, founded in Lambeth, South London in 1769. By the 1780s Coade stone was all the rage; the more ambitious Coade pieces were actually signed 'Coade of Lambeth', and Eleanor frequently employed the accomplished sculptor John Bacon to execute the larger works. Unfortunately, following the death of Eleanor Coade's daughter in 1821 and the subsequent closure of the Coade factory, the production of this unique product was discontinued. Even today, however, observers cannot but admire how well elements executed in this extremely tough and long-lasting material have weathered.

GENERAL REPAIRS

Before beginning any repair work, it is useful to remember that any apparent failure of, or damage to, an area of render does not mean that all of the wall's render needs to be replaced. Indeed, it is important to retain as much of the original material as possible – which, if it is still doing its job, should preferably be left alone.

Render should not be thought of as an unsympathetic method of covering up attractive walling materials. It is a vital element in the construction, and in the aesthetic effect, of countless Georgian properties. Removing old render from a wall, thereby revealing irregular masonry that was never intended to be seen by the original designer, often produces results that are visually ludicrous as well as structurally harmful.

On the right, a stone-built house in Tetbury, Gloucestershire, with its protective coat of pigmented limewash intact. On the left, all traces of the limewash have been removed – robbing the masonry of a shield against the weather as well as an aesthetically attractive finish – and the stone has been ribbon-pointed in cement.

If repairs are necessary, it is best to use a render of the same basic formula and strength as that already on the wall. Most importantly, care must be taken to avoid applying hard and brittle, cement-based render mixes onto Georgian buildings. Such coverings are denser than their traditional predecessors, and are impervious to water; if a crack in the render occurs as a result of wall movement or contraction caused by frost, incoming rainwater is unable to evaporate out again, condenses behind the cement and, with the first frost, freezes, expands and forces the render off the wall. At the same time, moisture also seeps back into the vulnerable masonry behind, trying to find an easier route for evaporation, and may cause serious internal damp problems (in particular, the rotting of structural timber and decay of the internal plasterwork through the action of harmful salts).

With any repair, ensure that the material your builder or craftsman is using matches the existing render in terms of composition and colour. A number of sources will be able to analyse render composition for you, so that an exact match of proportions and aggregates can be made. If the render is self-coloured, match the original using different coloured sands rather than artificial pigments, which will fade and discolour.

NEW RENDERS

It is always best not to render Georgian walls which were never intended to be covered by any such protective layer. (The only exception is when serious erosion due to severe weather conditions is a major problem.) A common modern fad is to cover perfectly sound and interesting brick walls with a cement-based render. Not only does this hide the textures and colours of the brickwork under a bland and unsympathetic coating, but, as noted above, it can also cause serious structural damage.

The ghastly visual effect that such modern coatings can have on old brick walls is particularly pronounced in the case of modern fake stone cladding. Stone cladding is generally either anchored with so much cement that it is impossible to remove it without tearing off most of the brickwork behind, or is so poorly fixed that component parts can fall onto passers-by. If applied to an old home, both cement rendering and stone cladding can substantially depress, rather than enhance, the retail value (as well as the historic worth) of the property.

LIME RENDER AND LIMEWASH

Lime, a versatile and immensely useful building material, has been produced for centuries using the same basic method. First, limestone is burnt in a kiln; then the resultant 'quicklime' is slaked with water (creating a hot and violent reaction in the process). The end result is 'lime putty', a soft material which needs to be stored for at least two weeks before use, but which can be used months after its slaking if kept in the right conditions.

'Lime mortar' (used for pointing brickwork or stonework) and 'lime render' (used for covering external or possibly internal walls) are made by mixing lime putty with a proportion of sand, and on occasion other aggregates, to produce what is called 'coarse stuff'. This has to be remixed (a process which in Britain is termed 'knocking up') before final use.

Lime render should always be used for historic structures in preference to modern, cement-rich render mixes. Unlike the latter, lime render allows the wall to 'breathe', which is vital if the structural integrity of the building is to be properly maintained.

Many builders will themselves need advice in repairing original Georgian renders, and particularly in finding the correct materials. It is not difficult to obtain the basic ingredients: lime putty is available from a variety of suppliers across the country, a selection of whom are listed on page 229. John Ashurst's English Heritage guide (*Mortars, Plasters and Renders,* 1988) also has a list of national lime suppliers. Other, more local sources can be recommended by your district council planning department's conservation officer.

If a colour wash or thin protective coating is required for your render or bare masonry, the best treatment is the traditional one: limewash. Limewash is easily made using lime putty and water; a simple, step-by-step account of the process can be found in the SPAB's comprehensive Information Sheet (see Further Reading, page 233). An alternative, traditional coating is copperas. This is still available from some outlets, and comes in three types: green copperas (based on ferrous sulphate), which produces a radiant, golden wash; blue copperas (based on copper sulphate), which can be used to produce a variety of blue or green tints (also called 'verditers'); and white copperas (from highly toxic zinc sulphate), which is often used to give a deeper tone to East Anglian 'white' brickwork.

STUCCO

Stucco was usually applied in three coats. The final application was flattened with a wood float and, as it began to set, was often lightly incised to resemble blocks of finely dressed stone.

A fine, stuccoed, late Georgian elevation from Saffron Walden in Essex.

Rendered ground floors in London's Bloomsbury. The render – like the railings, the first floor balconies and the altered windows – was added in the early 19th century.

In repairing stucco, ensure that the materials used in the mix produce a finish of a colour, texture and strength similar to the existing wall. As with any application of render, each coat should be progressively weaker (i.e. using more lime and fewer additions) than the one below. And make sure that any pattern of straight, incised lines which remain are copied in the new work – the damaged area having previously been cut back to the nearest 'joint' line.

Most stucco was intended to be painted. Yet the light cream tones we inevitably associate with stucco terraces today are actually a mid-19th-century innovation. Later Georgian or Federal stuccoes were originally coloured far darker than they appear today, since they were intended to reflect the hues of local stone. Outside London, pale greens, pale blues and, in East Anglia, robust pinks – colours generally based on local, naturally occurring pigments – are still widely used to colour rendered or stuccoed walls.

Stuccoville: St Andrew's Place, part of John Nash's Regent's Park development of the 1820s.

Stuccoed terraces were always conceived as unified compositions both in terms of style and colour. Today, even if the colour of the stucco no longer resembles that of the original facade, the same colour should always be adopted for the whole of the ter-

Stuccoed masonry, incised to suggest rusticated stonework.

race or block. These days responsible local authorities such as Hove and Westminster Councils actually stipulate the precise paint colour (using standard BS numbers) to be used on stuccoed surfaces. This helps to avoid unsympathetic 'individual' interpretations of adjoining houses.

Originally, too, the incised lines on the stucco which suggest stone joints were often enhanced by painted, grey 'shadows', while artists were also employed to give the stucco 'stones' a venerable, weathered look. Such *trompe-l'oeil* detail is today often submerged under layers of crude modern paint; where it does exist, however, get a recommended craftsman to restore it as sensitively as possible.

9

Wood Siding or Weatherboarding

WOOD SIDING HAS been used for centuries in areas where stone, or the materials needed to make bricks, were rare, yet wood was plentiful. As such, it is particularly prevalent along coastlines, most notably on the New England coast and, in Britain, on the coast of East Anglia (where this type of wall construction is called weatherboarding). Clearly, seaside communities which were largely dependent on fishing were very adept at working with interleaved wooden planking for boat-building, and their craft could be adapted to houses with ease.

In most cases wood boarding was applied in horizontal layers or courses to the exterior of a house. However, some instances of vertical boarding do survive. American 'board and batten' siding comprises vertical planks held in place by thin wooden battens which have been laid on top of the main boards.

In the US, the principal elevation of a wood-boarded house was often provided with a more subtle form of siding, more evocative of regular masonry courses. 'Flatboarding' or 'shiplap' – flush boards, fixed with close-fitting rebates or lap joints – was often used in this context; by way of a contrast, the side elevation was usually finished with a more rough-and-ready boarding technique. To help keep the flush-fitted boards as closely and neatly packed as possible, planks were often provided with a bottom edge thinner than that at the top; this arrangement is called 'bevel siding' or 'clapboarding' in the US, although in Britain the latter term is generally used to denote any type of boarded covering. A common American variation on flush boarding was 'drop siding', where tongued and grooved boards actually interlocked, giving even better protection from the elements. Overlapping boarding fastened in a similar fashion – linked by means of a groove, into which fitted a projecting rebate (or 'rabbet', an older English term which has survived in America) – was termed 'rabbeted bevel siding' in America and 'weatherboarding' in Britain – again, though, the label 'weatherboarding' is often used indiscriminately in Britain to describe any wood siding type.

ABOVE: *Flush 'flatboarding' on the front and cheaper, overlapping boards on the side of a house in Salem, Massachusetts.*

OPPOSITE: *Weatherboarded Colonial: the Crowninshield-Bentley House in Salem. Begun in 1727, this house was moved to its present site from a nearby location in 1960.*

87

MAINTENANCE

Using overlapping wooden planks to cover the exterior of a timber frame is a very basic and straightforward form of construction. However, it is also one that can be easily misunderstood or abused. Below are a few tips on how to maintain and repair your siding – and what to avoid.

Evident wood decay does not mean that the whole element – or indeed the whole wall covering – has to be replaced. The affected area can be cut out by an experienced joiner, and a replacement section pieced in; this saves both the original structure and your money. To safeguard against future damage, check that the cause of the problem has been fully dealt with before effecting repair; at the same time, try to use treated wood for the repaired area, and, if the problem has been a serious one, insert fungicidal plugs into the old wood adjacent to it.

If parts of the wood siding are missing, or are too far gone to piece in repairs, then ensure that they are replaced with wood of the same species and profile. Do not be tempted to replace siding with 'traditional' products made from a modern material such as aluminium or plastic; the new area will never look like wood, and will react differently with age.

Wood siding was invariably painted. Paint not only decorates, but also provides invaluable protection for the wood from the elements. Wood siding needs to be regularly repainted – about once every two or three years – if it is to be properly defended from water or insect penetration. If you have to remove extant paint layers before applying new paint – and painting over peeling or blistering old paint will prove a complete waste of time – never use a blowtorch or a similarly open flame; too many house fires have been started in this way. Hot air or steam strippers are always preferable when dealing with wood.

Varnishing wood siding or weatherboarding may provide a similar degree of protection to paint; however, it results in a messy visual effect never intended by the original

This is not stucco, nor painted stonework, but wood siding, cut to look like ashlar, painted and then sanded to give the wood the rougher texture of stonework. This ingenious technique was used by President Washington at his Virginia home of Mount Vernon.

*New England
flatboarding. As with so
many aspects of the
Georgian house, more
expensive finishes or
techniques were invariably
restricted to those areas
which could be easily seen
by visitors or passers-by.*

designers of the house. Bare wood may look fine for a log cabin; for Georgian homes –
whether on a Suffolk river or the coast of Maine – the effect is wholly inappropriate.

If insulation is to be added to the cavity behind the wood siding, do ensure that it is
properly ventilated. Wooden walls are obviously susceptible to damp, and thus need to
be able to 'breathe' – i.e. allow moisture to pass in and out of the wall as freely as possible. Without venting the insulation will absorb water coming in through gaps in the
siding, a development which will lead to damp and ultimately to rot problems in the
wood on both sides. Installing metal or plastic products in place of the traditional
wood siding will not solve the problem, and is only likely to exacerbate it.

10

Windows

WINDOWS ARE INVARIABLY the aspect of the house's exterior that are noticed first. They are effectively the eyes of a building (eyes which are, of course, so easy to extinguish), and any major alteration in their form or colour significantly alters the disposition of the facade. They are often, too, the feature which best defines the 'Georgian' aspect of a house.

The quintessential Georgian window is the double-hung sash. Although medieval-style casement windows, generally opened by hinges at the sides, were still in use during the period, by 1720 the sash window had become ubiquitous in houses in both Britain and America, and proved the most popular form of window opening for the next two centuries. It seems likely that the sash was a British invention – oddly enough, an invention which did not spread further than America and Holland – and that the first examples appeared in about 1670. These early sashes tended to be 'single-hung': the upper frame was immovable, and only the lower light could be moved. By the mid-18th century, however, double-hung sashes, where both frames could move, were the norm, operating either vertically or, in some regional variations such as the 'Yorkshire sash', horizontally.

No Georgian windows were constructed to a standard size; nor were the individual window panes of one set of dimensions. The characteristic mid-Georgian sash window was usually of six-over-six or eight-over-eight panes; this form, however, was gradually replaced by windows, larger in size, which comprised four-over-four or even two-over-two panes. As the century progressed, window joinery became increasingly hidden from view, as a precaution against fire entering the house via the vulnerable woodwork. The 1709 Building Act stipulated that windows be recessed at least four inches behind the face of the wall. The 1774 Act went further, demanding that almost all of the external window joinery be hidden behind the masonry, with only the sill and the immediate frame of the sashes showing.

ABOVE: *Detail of an exposed sash box, painted in off-white 'stone colour', of a Virginian window of the 1730s. While this type of fire risk was restricted by London's Building Act of 1709, it was some time before the British provinces and the American colonies began to follow suit and to hide the joinery of the box frame behind a skin of masonry.*

LEFT: *Walnut-colour window joinery contrasts with the yellow stock brickwork and the bright red, gauged-brick window arch in Sion Road, a terrace of 1721 in Twickenham, Middlesex. White was by no means the rule for Georgian windows.*

91

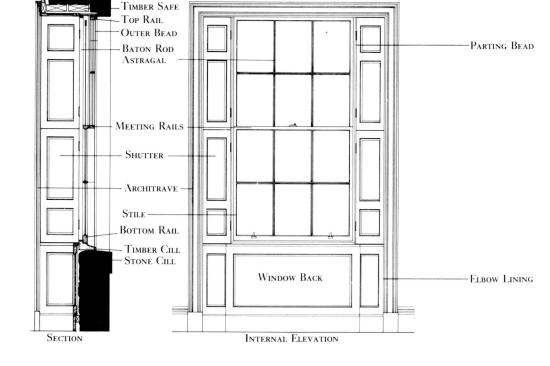

LINTEL
TIMBER SAFE
TOP RAIL
OUTER BEAD
BATON ROD
ASTRAGAL

PARTING BEAD

MEETING RAILS

SHUTTER

ARCHITRAVE

STILE

BOTTOM RAIL

TIMBER CILL
STONE CILL

WINDOW BACK

ELBOW LINING

SECTION

INTERNAL ELEVATION

ABOVE: *Cross-section of a sash box, from William Wilkins' St George's Hospital of 1826–9. The 'wagtail', the piece of wood which originally separated the two sash weights housed in this box, is missing. This element was rescued by Charles Brooking during the recent demolition of much of Wilkins' building; where this box was once installed now rise the pompous facades of the Lanesborough Hotel.*

The construction of the sash window was necessarily complex, so as to allow the two sashes to move with ease and to permit easy access to the sash boxes in the event of repair. To reach the sash cords and the side weights which counterbalanced each of the sash frames, the parting beads would be removed, enabling the removal of the sash frame as a whole and exposing the boxes which contained the cord-and-weight mechanism.

The internal glazing bars are often called 'astragals', or 'muntins' in the US; horizontal members are termed 'rails'; the two which overlap in the centre of the window, to which the sash fasteners could be fixed, are called 'meeting rails'. Each glazing bar is sinuously profiled inside the room, a plain rebate projecting through the glass to the exterior of the house.

WINDOW GLASS

A vital component of the Georgian window was, naturally enough, its glass. During the 18th century glass was generally made in one of two ways. 'Crown glass', the best quality product, was made by spinning out a blown globe of molten glass – a process which one contemporary observer described as 'a loud ruffling noise, like the rapid unfurling of a flag in a strong wind' – to form a disk not exceeding five or possibly six feet in diameter. This was then rested on a bed of sand, disengaged from the rod (or 'pontil'), and after cooling was cut into panes, the size of which could economically be no more than 10 in x 15 in. 'Cylinder', 'broad' or 'muff' glass was made by swinging the molten glass over a pit to lengthen it; the resulting cylinder was then opened out by reheating it over a metal plate covered in sand, and cut up into panes of rather more indifferent quality than could be achieved by the crown method.

All American window glass was imported from Britain until well after the Revolution. Some types of glass were made in the colonies from the mid-18th century, but the first window-glass factory was not set up until 1787, in Boston. American glass manufacture only became a truly successful concern after the war of 1812–14.

Old glass, particularly crown glass, is irreplaceable. Until recently, no British or American firm had manufactured glass in this manner since the 1930s, although a number of European and American firms do produce tolerable substitutes. However, as of spring 1992 crown glass is now once again being made in Britain. Hopefully, its high initial cost will be reduced as more customers are found.

When overhauling old windows, every effort should be made to retain original glass where it exists. Its faint greenish colour, its bell-like sound, and above all its marvellous oscillations and regular imperfections, which catch the light so beautifully, contrast dramatically with the dull, characterless uniformity of modern glass. If you are restoring old windows, make sure, then, that the glass is not unnecessarily replaced; so much crown or cylinder glass, despite initial assurances to the contrary from the builder, ends up in pieces on the skip.

By 1830 traditional glassmaking methods had been refined so as to allow for ever larger panes to be cut from the disks or cylinders. In 1832, however, the industry was irreversibly transformed: Lucas Chance began to produce a markedly improved form of cylinder glass at his factory in Stourbridge, using new continental techniques to produce the first 'plate' glass. This new, more standardized product revolutionized the industry and enabled the production of far larger panes of glass.

Innovations in glassmaking had immediate repercussions for the window-making trades, since windows could now be constructed without the heavy, substantial glazing bars previously needed to support the vulnerable glass. Thus the heavy ovolo glazing bar profiles of the early 18th century gradually gave way to more slender and graceful mouldings such as the ever-popular 'lamb's tongue' or 'Gothic' configurations. The introduction of stronger, metal glazing bars in the 1820s allowed for even fewer internal window supports.

ABOVE *top: Lamb's tongue and ogee glazing bar profiles, typical of Edinburgh homes of the second half of the 18th century. Below: a lamb's tongue moulding on a Late Georgian glazing bar.*

LEFT: *Manufacturing crown glass at Wakefield, Yorkshire, for Historic Building Services. The pioneering Wakefield venture produces the first British crown glass made for sixty years. Here the newly created circular 'table' is being enlarged in the furnace; when sufficiently wide – about four feet in diameter – it will be 'annealed' (slowly cooled) in an oven.*

Mid-Georgian sashes illuminating a cosily furnished first floor drawing room. By the end of the 18th century sash window openings – extant, early Georgian windows as well as new examples – were often being extended right down to ground floor level.

The introduction of plate glass meant that by 1840 sash windows could be made with no internal glazing at all. As a structural precaution, though, 'horns' were introduced at the corners of the meeting rails. Extensions of the stiles (the principal side members), they were designed specifically to strengthen the frames; they do not – as is often the practice with reproduction windows today – need to be added to Georgian windows, which have sufficient internal glazing bars to support the glass.

The bow window was certainly much used throughout the period. In seaside towns it was used to catch the sunlight radiating from the sea; inland, it was more often used as a device to front ground floor shops than to display the wares of non-commercial householders. (Even then, the 1774 Building Act stipulated that bay windows should project no further into the street than ten inches, and less in narrower lanes.) However, the 'bottle-glass bow' window – a feature so beloved of the purveyors of modern mock-Georgian – never truly existed. 'Bottle glass' or, more properly, 'bullion' panes were actually inferior by-products of the manufacture of crown glass, cut from the point of the spun circle where the glassblower's pontil had been affixed and later removed. Since glass remained an expensive commodity, even the centre of the crown circle was used; but most often the resulting pane was confined to windows which would never be glimpsed by passers-by: rear or kitchen windows, or perhaps modest internal doors leading into the kitchen. 'Bottle-glass' was never used on front elevations. There is, incidentally, evidence that these panes can represent serious fire hazards: the 'bottle-glass' indentation can concentrate the sun's rays in the manner of a magnifying glass and can actually set alight the curtains behind the window.

The natural progression from the extension of the window area was to convert the floor-length window into a glazed door – hence the 'French window'. Floor-length

Technological improvements in glass manufacture during the Regency period allowed joiners to experiment with more exotic forms and patterns. Here are two examples of the period: (left) margin lights in north London, and (right) a handsome Gothic opening in Ludlow.

windows or glazed doors were particularly used to give access into the garden at the rear of the house, or out onto newly fashionable features such as the ground floor conservatory or first floor verandah. Jane Austen's *Persuasion* (published in 1818, but written two or three years earlier) testifies to the popularity of this arrangement, eulogizing 'Uppercross Cottage, with its Viranda, French windows, and other prettiness'.

Whereas the panes of Regency windows were larger than before, visual interest was frequently retained by the device of inserting margin lights – narrow panes, placed at the borders of the glazing. These were often of coloured glass: pink, lilac, blue or amber. Indeed coloured glass became a feature of many Regency homes; Sir John Soane in particular delighted in using amber glass throughout the windows of his house in Lincoln's Inn Fields, thereby flooding the interior with glowing, radiant yellow light.

Another fancy, popular throughout the Georgian period, was Gothic glazing. Georgian 'Gothic' windows were not designed to be exact facsimiles of medieval examples, and were generally inserted into highly Classical contexts. By 1800 the smaller lights in these windows were often filled with coloured glass.

SASH FURNITURE

Technological advances affected not only the shape of the windows and the glass of the panes, but also the actual mechanisms within the sash boxes. In sophisticated houses rope sash cords were, from the 1820s onwards, replaced with tougher metal chains. More commonly, wooden sash pulleys – the rule for windows until the 1760s – were discarded in favour of longer-lasting examples made of brass or cast iron. Window furniture became more profuse and more elaborate, as brass and other alloys became cheaper and more widely available, and the fitting of devices such as sash fasteners became the rule rather than the exception.

An early 18th-century iron sash fastener from The Brooking Collection. This delightful example is far removed from most of the bright, brassy 'Georgian' window furniture available today.

RIGHT: *Window shutters at the John Marshall House, Richmond, Virginia of 1791.*

BELOW: *Tripartite sash window at Thomas Jefferson's Monticello, Virginia, completed in 1809.*

EXTERNAL SHUTTERS AND STORM WINDOWS

Georgian sashes were invariably fitted with internal shutters. (These are discussed below, in chapter 21.) Many houseowners are, however, unaware that they still possess workable shutters inside their shutter boxes. It is always worth checking this before you embark on complicated draughtproofing or secondary glazing.

Exterior shutters were to be found throughout the Georgian era. In Britain, most have now been dismantled, and only their fixtures survive as a record. (From the pictorial evidence which survives, it appears that these shutters were often painted a dark colour such as green.) On the east coast of the United States, however, the tradition of external shutters has largely survived intact. These were formerly used to protect the vulnerable windows from the ravages of the weather, but during the 20th century increasingly effective storm windows have been fulfilling this function, relegating external shutters to a purely decorative role.

If new shutters are to be fitted, ensure that they are substantial enough to be operated properly, even if they are largely intended as decoration, and that they can wholly cover the window openings when closed. Storm windows should be as unobtrusive as possible, both in terms of design and colour. If they are to be used to protect double-hung sash windows, check that the meeting rail in each sash corresponds to that in the two-part storm window which covers it. Storm windows fitted inside the main window provide the latter's glazing with little protection from the elements; however, if the elevation is a particularly sensitive one, which will be easily marred by the effect of externally sited storm windows, then internal installation may be the best bet.

External roller blinds were also decidedly popular on both sides of the Atlantic during the Late Georgian or Federal period. These were drawn up into painted wooden blind boxes, but while the boxes often survive – used as shades for the sun – it is extremely rare to find an extant exterior blind. From the evidence we do have, it seems that they were made of very heavy-duty canvas, and were often decorated in gaily coloured stripes.

Window Paint Colours

Georgian window colours varied far more than is often believed. For much of the 18th century window joinery was painted white or another light colour. (Georgian 'white', of course, was never akin to the bright, bleached whites so amenable to modern tastes; these stark whites are very much a product of the 20th century, being far too strident and dominating to be used on historical facades. Georgian whites were nearly always 'broken' – mixed with a tiny proportion of darker paints to give a richer effect; the result was often called not simply 'white' but 'stone colour'.)

By the 1780s, however, some windows, particularly when in the context of painted stucco, were painted in darker hues. The architect John Yenn employed dark grey windows in a villa design of 1769, while William Chambers used grey windows at Somerset

Early Georgian windows in Wilkes Street, Spitalfields, London with the spire of Nicholas Hawksmoor's contemporary Christ Church in the background. The swept-head window frames seen on the right, which needed additional work by the joiner to achieve the segmental curves, were inevitably more expensive than the regular, rectangular architraves seen on the left. Thus by the middle of the 18th century, segmental heads had largely been abandoned in favour of the simpler, rectilinear form. This view clearly demonstrates that brilliant white and pillar-box red, both very much colours of the 20th century, are inappropriate for Georgian facades.

99

House in London a few years later. And by 1800 darker greys and browns were surprisingly popular for fashionable homes. Soane frequently used dark painted sashes, while the leases of Nash's Regent's Park development specifically called for the repainting of the windows in a brown, imitation oak graining every four years. Green, too, was used for Regency window joinery, particularly in rural 'cottages ornées' and other products of the taste for the Picturesque.

Many of these darker colours were overpainted with cream as a result of the late 19th-century fashion for the chaste 'Queen Anne' style, and very few have survived the 20th century's rather disturbing passion to have everything whiter than white. Where there is no evidence for a darker colour, however, it is perhaps better to play safe and use a broken white for window joinery.

REPAIR OR REPLACEMENT?

In recent years plastic (PVC-U) and metal windows have become more widespread as a result of intense and aggressive marketing. In particular, the understandable wish to reduce fuel bills has been used as an excuse to rip out existing Georgian sashes and to replace them with plastic or metal products which incorporate double glazing. Such double glazed windows, however, not only look out of place in a Georgian facade, but may also represent the least cost-effective way of insulating an old house.

The government's official Planning Policy Guidance note no. 15 – the touchstone for countless British conservationists – specifically states that 'the insertion of factory-made standard windows of all kinds, whether in timber, aluminium, galvanised steel or plastic is almost always damaging to the character and appearance of historic buildings'. So-called 'Georgian-style' replacement windows generally have little in common with the Georgian timber sashes they replace, the character of the original openings often being wholly lost and replaced by ludicrous, two-dimensional parodies of Georgian models. The 'meeting rails', together with the other mass-produced members which are meant to suggest genuine joinery, are usually far too large and disproportionate. And when the new windows are opened, the visual effect is even worse.

Manufacturers frequently rely on misleading terminology to sell their wares, associating (in the case of windows) the concept of wood with that of inevitable decay, and stressing the advanced technology of PVC-U plastic and aluminium. Misleading claims regarding longevity and maintenance which arise from such marketing strategies pose a serious threat to genuine historic features and to the properties in which they are found. Equally worrying from the Georgian Group's point of view is the deliberate abuse of historical terminology in order to give poorly designed modern products and relatively untried modern materials the veneer of historical respectability. A 'Georgian' or, more insidiously, a 'Georgian-style' window is often little more than a bleach-white plastic frame with an internal grid of intersecting white, plastic strips. Nor is this approach limited to plastic: modern aluminium and stained hardwood windows are also often promoted as 'historic' products. The result of such misleading marketing is that terms such as 'Georgian' or 'Regency' are wholly devalued. At the same time, this hijacking of history even mixes periods, for instance providing 'Georgian' plastic window units with strips of 'diamond-pane leading' in a 'Tudor' style.

Generally fashioned as extremely crude approximations of Georgian sashes, replacement details such PVC-U plastic windows have not, despite the salesman's claims, been fully tried by time. What is often forgotten is that Georgian sashes have generally lasted 200 years or more, and, unlike their plastic rivals, can be repaired piecemeal (and cheaply) by an amateur, and – again, in contrast to pre-formed plastic units – be painted any colour you wish.

Plastic windows clearly remain a totally inadequate substitute for softwood fenestration. Information recently provided by the German government indicates that the life expectancy of such plastic window units is proving remarkably short: as little as five years for the fittings, and perhaps as little as twenty years for the plastic itself, which is exhibiting distinct tendencies to warp and discolour with age. Thus the arguments for easier maintenance and greater longevity of plastic windows appear to have little foundation in fact. Additionally, PVC-U is, unlike wood, a non-renewable resource: its manufacture is environmentally unsound and it can produce dioxins when burnt. More practically, the fitting of sealed double glazing units often necessitates the installation of extra ventilation for the masonry. And of course, by using local joiners to repair, rather than to replace, old windows, houseowners are providing a badly needed boost both to traditional craftsmen and to local industry.

There are good alternatives to double glazing: secondary glazing and draughtproofing are both highly effective remedies, while piecing in repairs to both windows and doors is always far cheaper, as well as far more sympathetic, than wholesale replacement. (For further information on this subject, the SPAB's highly informed technical pamphlet on *The Repair of Wood Windows* details simple and cheap alternatives to the philosophy of instant replacement.)

In summary, the key issue with regard to new windows in historic buildings is that unsuitable replacements can not only look hideous, but can also seriously diminish the value of a house, both through the structural damage they can cause and through the resultant disappearance of sought-after 'period' characteristics.

Secondary glazing installed in a Georgian house. Secondary glazing not only allows for the retention of the original sashes, but is far more effective than double glazing at reducing noise (the Building Research Establishment recommends at least a 10cm air gap between the two panes of glass in order to effectively eliminate noise) and even heat loss.

Doors

O LD FRONT DOORS have, in recent years, been much abused, yet they are of fundamental importance as the focus of any domestic facade. And, of all historic doors, perhaps the best-loved – and most-quoted – form is the Georgians' inimitable contribution to door development: the panelled front door.

Before the 18th century most doors were ledged: interlinked planks were bound with horizontal ledges or ties. By the early 18th century, however, the panelled door had become standard for all houses of any importance.

The panelled door which we so readily associate with Georgian houses consisted of a combination of panels, rails (horizontal members) and stiles (vertical members). The panels were either recessed or raised; if raised, they were also 'fielded' (provided with a chamfered edge). The number of panels in a door varied widely. The classic, typically Early Georgian arrangement was six panels, all disposed in accordance with the strict Palladian principles of proportion – that is, with the top two far smaller than the middle two, which were themselves slightly taller than the bottom two. (This disposition is, of course, very similar to that of the windows on each floor of a typical Palladian street elevation.) However, the pairs of panels would often be joined together, creating a door with five, seven or even just three panels. (The two bottom panels were frequently fused together and raised flush with the surrounding members to provide a thicker surface more resilient to impatient feet.) By the end of the 18th century three- and two-panelled front doors were common, often provided with added applied decoration in the form of raised circles or lozenges or, in the case of the classic Regency two-panelled front door, incorporating tall, round-headed panels running from top rail to bottom rail. Multiple bead mouldings ('reeded surrounds') were by the early 19th century often used to define the edges of the panels in internal doors, with paterae (each inset with a circular panel or similar motif) emphasizing the corners of the door, of the surrounding architrave, or just of each panel.

OPPOSITE: *Door and doorcase of the 1720s, from Sion Road, Twickenham. Note the heavy keystone and gap left for a rudimentary fanlight. Contrast the panelled door with the medieval ledged doorway from Clerkenwell, above.*

103

As the 18th century progressed doors became more substantial, while door mouldings became lighter and more subtle and door furniture increasingly delicate and elaborate. In 1749 the architect John Wood noted that, whereas in the 1720s 'the Doors were thin, and the best Locks had only Iron coverings varnished', by the late 1740s in grander homes 'the Doors in general were not only made thick and substantial, but they had the best Sort of Brass Locks put on them.'

EXTERNAL DOORCASES

Doorcases of the early 18th century were often of the hood and bracket form, their boldly projecting outlines, weighty hoods and imaginatively carved supporting brackets or scrolls reflecting the dramatic Baroque enthusiasms of the time. During the 1720s, however, these Baroque examples began to give way to what soon became the orthodox Palladian temple-front or 'aedicular' doorcase. This arrangement – columns, pilasters or implied pilasters on either side of the door supporting a simple pediment or lintel entablature – became the standard pattern for the remainder of the Georgian period.

FANLIGHTS

Fanlights first began to appear in the 1720s, and were quickly assimilated into the typical Palladian doorcase format. Not only did they allow light to enter the hall or corridor behind; they also provided the designer with great scope for individuality, and were as a result highly popular with the mid-18th-century practitioners of the elaborate and sophisticated Rococo and Adam styles.

In Britain the 1760s and 1770s were the great age of the fanlight. (In America the Adam-style fanlight did not become widely accepted until the 1780s.) Fanlights of the

Adam period were large, complex compositions of iron and lead, whose intricate tracery extended across the whole width of the doorcase. By 1800, however, the delicate tracery of the 1770s had been largely replaced with more prosaic designs, based on simple geometric shapes or – a form particularly characteristic of the early 19th-century doorcase – serpentine curves. The 'teardrop' or 'batswing' designs of the 1820s and 30s, far flatter and considerably less intricate that their predecessors of fifty years before, are particularly well-known examples of this type.

By the 1840s leaded fanlights had become less fashionable, as glass began to be inserted into the body of the door itself. Single-sheet lights, far stronger than traditional leaded forms, became especially popular following the introduction in 1832, by Chance Brothers of Stourbridge, Worcestershire, of good quality plate or 'broad' glass, which did not need any internal glazing bars, muntins or leading to make it structurally secure.

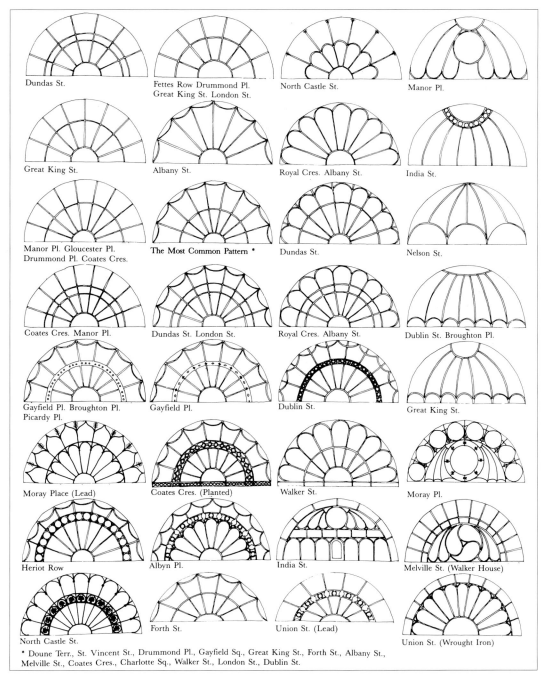

Late 18th-century fanlights from Edinburgh's New Town, featuring both the more traditional, delicate, Adam-style tracery and the newer, batswing and teardrop designs. From Edinburgh New Town Conservation Committee's excellent design manual, The Care and Conservation of Georgian Houses *(Butterworth, 3rd edition, 1986).*

Dundas St.

Fettes Row Drummond Pl. Great King St. London St.

North Castle St.

Manor Pl.

Great King St.

Albany St.

Royal Cres. Albany St.

India St.

Manor Pl. Gloucester Pl. Drummond Pl. Coates Cres.

The Most Common Pattern *

Dundas St.

Nelson St.

Coates Cres. Manor Pl.

Dundas St. London St.

Royal Cres. Albany St.

Dublin St. Broughton Pl.

Gayfield Pl. Broughton Pl. Picardy Pl.

Gayfield Pl.

Dublin St.

Great King St.

Moray Place (Lead)

Coates Cres. (Planted)

Walker St.

Moray Pl.

Heriot Row

Albyn Pl.

India St.

Melville St. (Walker House)

North Castle St.

Forth St.

Union St. (Lead)

Union St. (Wrought Iron)

* Doune Terr., St. Vincent St., Drummond Pl., Gayfield Sq., Great King St., Forth St., Albany St., Melville St., Coates Cres., Charlotte Sq., Walker St., London St., Dublin St.

RIGHT: *Pediment, carved frieze and brackets from a doorcase of 1734 in Stoke Newington, North London. Not all of this woodwork is original: the doorcase was stolen in 1982, and only parts – including a bracket and the central face mask – were recovered from a skip by the local Conservation Officer.*

BELOW RIGHT: *A fine internal doorway with a 'Gibbs surround' – a prominent keystone and block quoins punctuating the architrave – from Salisbury, Wiltshire.*

OPPOSITE: *Another Salisbury doorcase, this time with an open pediment boldly projecting into the hall's cornice.*

A rare, glazed internal doorway of the mid-18th century from Islington in north London.

INTERNAL DOORS

In most cases before 1840 only internal doors were glazed – particularly those leading in and out of the kitchen, where the glass had an obvious practical benefit. In these instances four or perhaps nine panes of glass would be inserted into the top half of the door. On occasion the indented central portion of the crown glass disc could be used.

DOOR FURNITURE

Georgian door furniture is an area where there are many misconceptions. Despite what many modern manufacturers of 'period' products are keen to suggest, during the 18th century fittings for front doors were most often made not of brass – an expensive commodity before the Industrial Revolution – but of cast iron, painted black. Before the early 19th century the only element of door furniture generally used was the door knob – perhaps augmented by a simple, hefty knocker. Front door knobs were usually situated at waist height, in the centre of the middle or lock rail. Letter boxes were, of course, a mid-Victorian innovation – the British postal system only truly began in 1840

– while door numbers were used only sporadically during the early decades of the 19th century (although mandatory in London after 1805).

Shiny, modern fittings are often quite inappropriate for a Georgian door. Perhaps worse than their crude, ahistorical design is the tendency to use such models to dominate the front door to an excessive degree. The Georgian door was never meant to be a backcloth for a panoply of shiny brass fittings; the unsubtle brightness and thin superficiality of many modern brass products tend to obscure the aesthetic worth of the front or internal doors to which they are attached. They can also be a historical nonsense: for instance the ubiquitous 'Adam' urn-shaped brass knocker, never actually used by Adam, or the lever-operated doorhandles which were rarely used on any door before the 20th century.

During the second half of the 18th century, simple, functional rim locks (i.e. locks applied to the exterior of the door and door architrave) began to be replaced with iron, steel or brass 'mortise' locks, which operated within the fabric of the door itself. In 1784 Joseph Bramah invented the first door lock opened with a key which was not heavy and ponderous but small and easily pocketable; the lock itself was operated by the action of a rotating barrel and not via the traditional sliding bolt – an innovation further perfected in

Elevation

A hybrid internal door from Rowallan Old Castle, Ayrshire. From Colin Amery's Three Centuries of Architectural Craftsmanship *(Butterworth, 1977).*

the 1840s in the form of the classic Yale cylindrical lock. In 1818 the Chubb lock was patented, a device whose mechanism was able to detect tiny variations in key patterns.

It is clearly important to retain all original knockers, hinges, locks, numbers and other items of door furniture if you do have to repair or remove old doors. This advice applies as much to the simplest internal door as to the grandest front entrance. Georgian iron hinges, for example, are quite irreplaceable, so do not be tempted to replace them with purely decorative strap-hinges which hide modern hinge mechanisms. Even if the Fire Officer insists that door locks be altered to enable the doors to be self-closing, save the original door furniture and ensure that any new additions are as subtle, discreet and sympathetically proportioned as possible. If new locks are to be fitted, try to ensure that they are, at least on the outside, duplicates of what was there before.

MODERN 'PERIOD' DOORS

Many modern examples of the door manufacturer's art – whether designated 'period', 'traditional' or 'Georgian-style' – actually have very little in common with the original designs they are supposed to mimic, yet they are frequently inserted into Georgian homes in the mistaken belief that they are aesthetically and historically appropriate. If they have been used to replace original doors in a listed building, this can actually result in a legal prosecution, as Listed Building Consent is necessary for such a major alteration. And even if the house is not a listed property, the substitution of ersatz-historical features for genuine ones can seriously reduce the financial value of the building.

Two basic misconceptions about Georgian doors should be quickly demolished. Firstly, the modern fad for 'slipped fanlight' doors – front or rear doors which have

Robert Adam door furniture from Osterley Park, Middlesex, a house remodelled for the banker Robert Child after 1763.

A delicate doorcase of the early 1770s, probably carved by William Buckland himself, from the dining room at the Hammond-Harwood House, Annapolis, Maryland.

111

crude 'fanlights' integrated within the body of the door – is not based on Georgian precedent. As we have already seen, glass only appeared in the body of the door during the Victorian era; before this, the Georgian door was in most cases totally separated from the glazed fanlight above. The only exception to this rule was the tendency in some regions to replace the two, upper panels of the door with glass, a practice which is still acceptable today.

The second major misconception is that wood, as used for architraves and panelling as well as external and internal doors, was left unadorned in the Georgian house. This is quite wrong, and appears to be based on a recent confusion of Georgian practice with 20th-century modernist theory and in particular with the post-war fashion for 'honest', stripped Scandinavian timber. Georgian doors were nearly always painted, and never left bare. Some humble internal doors, away from the principal rooms, may occasionally have been left unpainted, but even these would have been given repeated layers of wax polish. The Georgians recognized – while we have largely forgotten – that naked wood is easy prey to woodworm (whose larva finds paint impenetrable but uncovered timber delicious). And Georgian architects and builders would be shocked to see the inferior, knotty pine of internal doors stripped, having intended that this cheap material never actually be seen. When the exposed wood of a front door is a tropical hardwood from Brazil or the Philippines, then its use also becomes environmentally unsound.

Doors can be cheaply and easily repaired and brought up to modern environmental standards. Replacement should only be a last resort.

REPAIRING DOORS

If new hardwood is to be pieced in as part of a door repair, make sure this new wood has been properly seasoned before insertion, or it may distort. Warped doors can be easily remedied by planing. If bad draughts are a problem, a weathering strip can be inserted into the bottom of the door, which can also be grooved to catch rainwater (a corresponding lowering of the rebate outside ensuring that the water will subsequently flow away from the door). Weatherstrips are now widely available, and can keep out noise as well as draughts. For greater security, metal straps can be fixed to the inside of the front door in emulation of Georgian practice.

Remember that it is always best to leave internal doors in place, even if they are no longer in use. The alternatives – gaping holes, or ugly infill panels – can easily ruin the carefully wrought proportions of a room or hallway.

In the past, fire regulations have often been used as an excuse to remove or mutilate Georgian doors; this is generally avoidable, however. The British Fire Precautions Act states that doors should not be less than 45mm thick and that an internal door should have at least thirty minutes' fire resistance. Yet Georgian doors are usually solidly built: often the stiles and rails are thicker than 45mm, and it is a simple task for a competent joiner to attach new layers to the thinner panels or, better still, to split the panels and insert fire-resistant sheets in the middle like a sandwich. The use of 'intumescent paint', which expands to form a heat barrier while starving flames of oxygen, can also help.

The favourite solution of the 1960s and 70s to fire prevention – sticking a hideous hardboard or asbestolux cover over the whole door – has, thankfully, saved many old doors from destruction. Removing these unsightly layers will often expose marvellous Georgian mouldings.

REPAIRING PORCHES

Doorcases and porches are inevitably very susceptible to damp, particularly if the lead flashing has come adrift from the wall behind, and to tilting. Solving the latter is comparatively easy for a professional, who can provide a slip joint between the wall and the porch, underpin the porch and improve the foundations, or simply bind the porch more effectively to the masonry behind.

If porch mouldings need to be replaced, ensure that any existing details are repeated, and follow any regional variations or characteristics if these are relevant. If some elements or materials are unavailable – for example, Coade stone mouldings (see page 78) – then a faithful replica in plaster or masonry is the best solution.

Do not be tempted to suggest the addition of new details or designs for which there is no precedent. Historically inappropriate porches added to extant doorways always look new – and distinctly uncomfortable.

REPAIRING FANLIGHTS

Fanlights are still made in the traditional fashion – although many would-be improvers of Georgian houses are led to believe that the only alternatives available to them are the grotesque parodies which pose as genuine Georgian designs. If repairing or re-inserting a fanlight, take care to integrate the glass with the glazing bars or leading – fake bars or fake leading should not simply be stuck on the outside of the glass – and avoid the clumsy, patio-style 'wrought iron' designs that are becoming so prevalent.

Remember, it is always better to repair a damaged Georgian fanlight than to insert a lifeless modern reproduction – a principle which holds good everywhere in the Georgian home.

PAINTING DOORS

Doors and doorcases should be repainted about every three to four years, in order to prevent water from seeping in through damaged paintwork. Inevitably, successive repainting leads to a build-up of paint layers which must be removed sooner or later if the door mouldings are not to be wholly obscured. Paint layers can be removed by using hot air guns, gentle caustic solutions or liquid paint strippers; solutions that eat into wood, and particularly blowtorches, should be avoided.

Today doors are painted every conceivable colour. During the Georgian era, however, front doors appear to have been largely painted a dark colour – dark green or brown were especially popular – or on occasion 'grained' to imitate seasoned oak or other exotic woods. In contrast, the door surround was painted broken white or a light 'stone colour'. Internal doors tended to reflect the colour scheme of the room, or were painted in fashionable dark shades which matched the dark skirting – chocolate brown was a perennial favourite.

If original graining of the door (or marbling of the doorcase) still exists, then try to have it reproduced professionally. And if your house has gilding on the doorcase or even on the door itself, have this replicated by a professional, too. Cheap gold paint is never a good substitute for genuine gilding, since it dulls and tarnishes very quickly.

─────────── 〔12〕 ───────────

Roofs

W HEREAS PRE-GEORGIAN buildings invariably included prominent, high roofs, fashionable Georgian homes were designed so as to ensure that the roof itself remained hidden from view at street level, by placing the roofline parallel, not at right angles, to the high, street-front parapet. Many Georgian houses were provided with M-shaped roofs with valley gutters – the double pitch being needed to span the many rooms which ran away from the costly, and thus narrow, street front. These M-roofs have since caused many structural problems. Their valley gutters are all too easily choked with rubbish and debris, with the result that water penetrates into the house below.

A wide variety of roof coverings were used in the Georgian period: true slates, clay tiles, stone slates, timber shingles, thatch, copper and of course lead. Whatever covering you discover, it is always best – both aesthetically and structurally – to replace failed elements with the same basic material.

ABOVE: Westmorland slates laid in diminishing courses on a fine, early 18th-century M-shaped roof in Bury St Edmunds, Suffolk.

OPPOSITE: A mansard roof with prominent dormers and Dutch-influenced gable end on an early 18th-century brick house in Marlborough, Wiltshire.

THE DORMER WINDOW

The derivation of the term 'dormer window' is not hard to guess. It comes from the French *dormer*, to sleep, indicating that these windows were designed to light the roof-space – an area which, traditionally, was in most cases devoted exclusively to inferior sleeping accommodation. The roofspace was the hottest area of the house in summer, and the draughtiest in winter; as a result, this was always where the poorest members of the household – the servants – slept. And there was, of course, no reason why their windows had to be too large.

Dormers have existed for centuries wherever pitched roofs have occurred – i.e. generally in the more northerly countries of Europe and their colonies. Dormer windows were originally used during the later medieval period in Britain to light large rooms open to the roof, but by the end of the 16th century they were used to illuminate

115

RIGHT: *A decidedly exaggerated mansard roof, with rather over-emphasized dormers, in a Sussex house of the early 18th century.*

BELOW: *Equally prominent dormers at Woodlawn, Virginia.*

rooms created in the roofspace itself. These early examples were often in the form of so-called 'eyebrow' dormers – dormers which, in the context of a thatched or tiled roof, were protected not by their own pitched roof but by a small, undulating variation in the line of the overall roof covering.

The Dutch-influenced buildings of the later 17th century, with their steeply pitched roofs and their elaborate gables, inaugurated the golden age of the dormer window in Britain. In particular, the new, two-pitched 'mansard' roofs – named after the celebrated late 17th-century French architect François Mansard – proved particularly suited to the creation of rooms within the copious roofspace and to the corresponding provision of robust openings (see page 123). Large dormer windows, specifically designed to blend with the rhythm, scale and materials of the house below, thus became a prominent feature of those avant-garde, red-brick homes of the later 17th century and early 18th century, which took as their inspiration Roger Pratt's revolutionary designs for Coleshill and Kingston Lacy. Houses in this style continued to be built in America well into the 18th century.

With the introduction of the ostensibly flat-roofed houses at the end of the 17th century, the dormer disappeared from the most up-to-date great houses of Britain and America, as patrons learned to hide their fashionably low-pitched roofs behind tall parapet walls. However, the dormer remained in constant use in more modest homes – particularly in those situated in the heart of the town or village, where it was necessary to economize as far as possible on ground space.

The design for the principal elevation of a dormer window generally mirrored that adopted for the fenestration below. Thus Georgian dormers were usually provided with two-part sashes; the upper sash was often only one pane in depth, but in some instances six-over-six or even eight-over-eight pane sashes were installed in direct imitation of the full-sized windows in the wall below. The glazed area could be square or rectangular (and possibly pedimented), or given segmental heads. Some were even provided with bowed fronts.

The majority of dormers were traditionally designed to terminate in pitched roofs, running at right angles to the line of the main roof. Others were given a 'pent' roof, an outcrop of the main roof slope at a lower pitch. And while dormers mostly project from the plane of the roof, some can actually be found which have been recessed into the roof itself. When dormers were used in the context of a thatched roof, courses of tiles, extending down to the eaves guttering, were often placed directly below each individual dormer, in order both to help shed water more effectively and to protect the vulnerable thatch.

Countless local variations exist. In east London's Spitalfields district, for example, there are numerous multi-light dormers, later additions which were designed to illuminate the Early Georgian textile workshops. It is therefore always best to follow regional practice and tradition when seeking to repair or install dormers.

ROOF TILES

Clay tiles have been with us for centuries. The simplest clay tile, the peg or plain tile, is rectangular and almost flat, although often with a slight double camber to help shed water. Traditionally made examples, however, have an individual character and patina which modern mass-produced products fail to recapture. From the mid-19th century onwards tiles with regular, crisp edges were mass-produced by machine.

Plain tiles are punctured by two nail holes, used for fixing the tile to the wooden roof battens. Others can be provided with 'nibs', right-angled projections from which the tile can hang on the batten (see adjacent), which were originally formed by pushing the clay forward with the thumb. The pantile was a later, early 18th-century development: an S-shaped, nibbed product which could be interlinked with its fellows without the aid of wooden pegs or iron nails. Pantiles should not be confused with so-called 'Roman' tiles, whose semicircular or elliptical projections produce a far more regular and mathematical pattern than the gently curved pantiles. Also of semicircular shape were the special ridge tiles manufactured to cap the ridges at the top and hip of the roof.

Most 18th-century roofing tiles carried no maker's name; they were generally produced locally – and anonymously – by individuals or by small workshops. Thumb and finger prints are often the only clue to the identity of the maker; occasionally, too, you may be lucky enough to find a hand-incised date on the tile.

The manufacture of traditional plain tiles almost stopped completely in the 1930s. Today, thankfully, the industry has been comprehensively revived. Most traditional clay tile manufacture is now centred on the southeastern counties of Kent, Sussex and Hampshire, where many buildings still display fine examples of the tile-maker's art. Your local authority Conservation Officer can provide you with names of local suppliers of traditionally made clay tiles.

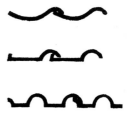

ABOVE: *Three different styles of tile, from top: plain tiles, Roman tiles and pantiles.*

BELOW: *Plain tiles being laid on wooden battens. It is vital to ensure proper ventilation of the underside of such roof coverings, without which corrosion and rot can easily occur.*

117

ROOF SLATES

Slate used as a roofing material was a common feature of slate-producing areas by 1700. Roof slates were not introduced into the capital and other major cities, however, until the mid-18th century. British slates – fixed by nailing into battens – come in four basic varieties: blue-grey slates from the Lake District; grey slates from mid-Wales; blue or rarer plum red slates from northwest Wales; and grey-green 'Delabole' slates from Cornwall. Imported slates are becoming increasingly common in Britain. However, while they are sometimes cheaper, their lifespan may be significantly shorter than British products; additionally, they may also weather in a considerably different manner from adjacent, native examples.

In some areas – for example, in the Lake District – slates (and stone 'slates') have traditionally been laid in diminishing courses, the size of the slate decreasing the nearer you get to the apex of the roof. This visually appealing arrangement transfers much of the weight of the roof covering to the strong outer walls, rather than to the fragile roof apex, and also provides a greater surface area from which the rainwater can run off – into the gutter or thrown well clear of the wall. Welsh slates, on the other hand, are often of uniform size. Whatever arrangement you find, it is always best to follow the local pattern.

STONE 'SLATES'

Stone slates are usually (though not always) found in areas with good local stone, and little or no slate or clay tile manufacture. They can vary greatly according to locality, from the old red sandstone slates of Herefordshire and Worcestershire, through the pale, fossil-riven Purbeck slates from the Dorset coast, to the perennially popular limestone slates – in particular the fawn-coloured Collywestons from the East Midlands and

Recently repaired Welsh slates on a Midlands roof. Foreign slate substitutes rarely perform as well as their Welsh or English equivalents: although often cheaper, they weather differently, and may not last long.

LEFT: *Diminishing courses of attractively weathered stone slates on an Oxfordshire roof.* BELOW: *Recovered stone slates in Gloucestershire.*

the golden Cotswolds from the Oxfordshire–Gloucestershire border. Some stone slates are actually exposed to frost to allow them to be split into workable sizes; others are simply mined and dressed to the requisite lengths. By the mid-20th century the mining of stone for traditional slates had almost ceased. Reassuringly, however, quarries are now reopening as the enthusiasm for historic roof coverings is rekindled.

LEADWORK

Sheet lead began to be used to make decorated 'heads' – used (instead of gargoyles) to catch rainwater from the roof and to disperse it in downpipes – in the 15th century. By the 17th century the decoration of both rainwater heads and the lead cisterns installed at ground level to hold the rainwater had become very ornate. A good number of the bulkier cisterns were made not by hammering or cutting sheet lead into various patterns, but by actually casting the tanks in sand beds impressed with carved moulds. Cisterns and rainwater heads are often of great help in determining when the building was completed, since the date is often prominently inscribed as part of the design.

Lead, copper or zinc flashings are an essential part of the roof, helping to ensure that the structure remains dry and safely protected by excluding water from the vital junctions between the roof covering and the gutters, dormers and walls. They should be examined regularly, and professionally inspected every five years. Today many lead flashings are replaced in zinc – which, though it has a shorter lifespan than lead, is also cheaper, and still lasts far longer than other alternatives. Cracks in both lead and zinc sheeting should not be soldered shut: this will simply prompt further cracking in the near future.

119

GENERAL ROOF REPAIRS

If you are contemplating roof repairs or alterations, it is helpful to bear a few simple rules in mind. Firstly, do not alter the roof so that it projects further (either higher or further forward) than that of its neighbours. Secondly, ensure that any repair or addition is in keeping with the existing forms and materials. Thirdly, if there is any original roof structure left, take care to see that this is preserved: you may not want it, but subsequent owners of the house may. It is also worth taking the opportunity of roof repair or maintenance to inspect every element of the roof structure while access is easily available. Roof inspections (both external and internal) should ideally be carried out every year, preferably after the autumn gales.

While much of the fabric of your house may be Georgian, or indeed post-Georgian, the roof structure may actually be pre-Georgian. If so, contact the SPAB (see Sources, page 228) for advice and information on how to repair old timber roofs.

In most cases, roof repair is such a tricky problem that it is always worth consulting a recognized expert – a qualified surveyor or architect – before you begin. This can prevent costly mistakes being made later on. Additionally, remember that, whatever type of material you use to cover your roof, if your house is listed, or if it is in a Conservation Area, you may need some form of local authority consent before you proceed. A useful rule of thumb is always to ask before you start; local district or borough council Conservation Officers, or experienced architects or surveyors, can be particularly helpful in this respect.

Guttering should always be kept free of plants and debris.

Detailed procedures for roof repairs can be found in the excellent Edinburgh New Town Conservation Committee manual and in other works cited on page 233.

TILING REPAIRS

Secondhand slates can be used to repair a slate roof as long as they have not deteriorated or softened too far and their nail holes have not been over-enlarged. (Many clay or slate tiles tend to 'delaminate' with age: the water penetrates the tile and causes it to split into layers.) However, it may be more cost-effective to buy a few new tiles, rather than spending weeks attempting to find suitably matching examples. If using either new or secondhand examples that are not exact matches, try and place the replacement tiles in areas which are not easily visible. Alternatively, try to scatter them about the old tiling so they do not form an instantly recognizable 'patch'.

When replacing tiles or slates, always ensure that the new tiling matches the existing work in terms of texture, size and colour as far as possible. On a practical note, remember that tiling repairs can be dangerous for passers-by – so make sure that no one is in the line of fire when tiles become dislodged and fall to the ground. (Be careful, too, of those who are working on the roof itself: roof structures are often more fragile than they look.)

If you have to replace all the existing tiles or slates, it may be helpful to lay down roofing felt first, if none exists already. This can give added weather protection. Take care, though, to ensure that the felt and the overlaid material is properly ventilated, otherwise condensation-related problems will occur. Felt may not be necessary (and may actually prove quite unsightly) if the tiling – say, on a front porch – is visible from below. Felt underlay is also generally inappropriate for stone roofs, since stone slates are often bedded in mortar.

Rotten battens should always be replaced, as should any of the old iron nails which have rusted away. Any new, replacement battens should be pre-treated against fungal attack, and fixed with stainless steel nails. New fixing nails for slates or tiles should preferably be non-ferrous: made of copper or, if this is unobtainable, of stainless steel – not iron or galvanized steel. If rare oak pegs were used and still survive, try to find a local supplier who can replace like with like.

Concrete tiles are quite unsuitable for historic buildings, in both appearance and the weight they bring to bear on a roof structure never intended to take such loads. A recent judgment by a Department of the Environment inspector at a public inquiry noted that 'the stark and brash appearance of the concrete tiles' in question bore 'no resemblance to the mellowed and weathered appearance of second-hand clay pantiles'. The tiles also, it was stated, contrasted unfavourably with the old brickwork below. As the inspector in this case – which concerned the re-roofing of listed farm outbuildings – sensibly concluded, 'conversion of traditional buildings must entail care, trouble and expense if their character and appearance is to be retained'. (Details of this case, a prosecution won by Newark and Sherwood District Council, can be found in the issue of *Context* magazine for June 1990.)

Cement fibre 'slate' or reconstituted stone tiles may initially appear a more acceptable substitute for the real thing than concrete products. The effect, however, is often equally unsightly. Such tiles inevitably look too new and, even if they have been provided with artificial 'weathering', too obviously machine-made. This effect will not necessarily disappear with weathering, as many of the lichens which give so much character to old roofs will not grow on these modern hybrids. Artificial products which purport to mimic real slates never convince and are always unacceptable.

When repairing failed tiling, it is never a good idea to try to bed your new tiles in mortar (unless this was originally used for stone 'slates'), or to cover the lot with tar, bitumen or a similar finish. Neither of these methods works as a means of preventing water penetration: if a roof needs repairing, no amount of 'sealing' – which generally results in an unsightly mess, and prevents the tiles being used again – will help eradicate the basic problem.

Methods of repairing or replacing stone-tiled roofs can be found in Adela Wright's recent guide to traditional materials, which also includes a list of modern suppliers of roofing slates and stone slates, while an excellent guide to timber roof repairs can be found in James Boutwood's SPAB technical pamphlet. (For both of these books see Further Reading, page 233–4.)

REPAIRING LEADWORK AND GUTTERING

The failure of lead roofs often stems from a simple problem – usually involving the incorrect fixing of the original sheets, exacerbated by the subsequent contraction and expansion of the metal. After a number of years, roofing lead – exposed as it is to great variations in temperature – will distort to an extent where it is of little practical use. It is then time to replace it. The Lead Development Association (see Sources, page 230) can advise on methods of repair, and on local suppliers. Whatever you do, never use

Typical Georgian roof section, assembled by P. & D. Trevor for The Building of Bath Museum. Note the camber of the coping and of the cornice, designed to throw water into the parapet gutter and the street respectively.

bitumen or other 'sealants' to repair cracks in leadwork; they fail to solve the problem in the long term, and are also difficult to remove at a later date. And always ensure that the lead sheeting has sufficient ventilation below – otherwise rapid corrosion can occur. Details of the treatment of leadwork and of other roof repairs can be found in the Edinburgh New Town conservation manual (see Further Reading, page 233).

Gutters and downpipes leading to and from rainwater heads were for much of the Georgian period made of softwood, sometimes lined with lead. By the end of the 18th century, however, many were being made from cast iron. If you can, always replace failed cast iron sections with pieces in the same material and shape. In some cases cast (not extruded) aluminium or copper can prove an acceptable alternative. It is always, however, worth having a rare timber gutter replaced in wood (usually elm) if you encounter one. Modern plastic gutters may be cheaper, but are often visually offensive as well as more susceptible to damage; nor is it really known how long they will last. And when fitting new metal downpipes, make sure that they are spaced far enough from the wall to allow the water to run down the pipe, rather than the more vulnerable masonry, in the event of a leak. This will also allow for easy repainting – and regular repainting is vital if the metal is to be properly protected from rust.

Remember, too, that it is vital that your guttering system is fully maintained and in perfect working order. Any failures may prompt serious structural harm as a result of water penetrating or saturating the masonry behind. Valley gutters are areas of especial concern; it is important that they are always kept free of rubbish or other impediments. One simple way of checking whether you have any gutter failures is to have a look round the outside of your home when it is raining heavily: any problems will be immediately, and wetly, obvious.

Some roofing may originally have been executed in copper rather than lead. In this case, although replacing like for like is always the best policy, the substitution of lead sheets may prove more economic.

REPAIRING SHINGLES

Fewer and fewer Georgian houses now retain their original wooden shingle roofs. If, however, you find your house still has one, try to replace any failed shingles with copies made of oak (or, failing that, imported sweet chestnut), fixed with copper nails. (Cedar shingles are rarely the correct size, or the correct texture and colour, to use in this context.) It is particularly important with this form of roof covering to ensure that there is sufficient ventilation to the roof – otherwise serious decay can occur.

REPAIRING THATCH

A thatched roof on a rural Georgian property can do much to enhance the building's character and value. It is therefore important to get any thatching repairs right. Ensure that you are using the correct type of material for your region – whether it is 'Norfolk reed' (made from water reeds), 'Devon reed' (from long straw), sedge, or other, rarer thatching materials. Details of the approach and methods to be followed when rethatching old properties can be found in the SPAB's excellent technical guide on this subject (see Further Reading, page 233).

REPAIRING CHIMNEYS

With the installation of central heating, many chimney stacks and flues are now redundant. However, it is important to leave them in place. Not only can the demolition of a chimney stack completely alter the visual balance of an individual facade, or even of a whole street; additionally, subsequent owners may want to use the fireplace again, and find that they are frustrated from doing so. Chimney stacks can also serve an important structural function, anchoring the walls and internal divisions, so any demolition can cause serious structural weaknesses. As with so many aspects of altering the Georgian or Victorian home for modern requirements, always ensure that any changes you make are fully reversible by later generations.

Ensure, too, that your chimney stack and chimneypot are well maintained. Any collapse will endanger not only your roof, but the rooms below, too. Full details of the repair of chimney stacks are given in G.B.A. Williams' SPAB technical pamphlet (see Further Reading, page 233).

ADDING A MANSARD ROOF

Mansard roofs, popular in Britain and America from the late 17th century onwards, can be defined as those roofs which have two, differently pitched slopes on each side – enabling additional accommodation to be inserted behind the lower, steeper slope. ('Gambrel' roofs are Mansards with an exposed gable at either end.) Today Mansards are commonly – perhaps too commonly – used in an attempt to prise even more use out of a traditional roofspace.

Mansard roofs can represent a highly attractive feature of a house. They are certainly infinitely preferable to the type of vertically pitched, asphalted coverings seen on many shoddily built attic additions of the post-war period. However, their spatial advantages, and in particular their ability to be punctuated by recurring dormer windows, are qualities which are frequently abused by less sympathetic architects and builders. Often the lower pitch of the Mansard is executed to rise almost vertically, its tile-hung exterior hiding what is effectively an additional floor – but one which, by posing as a roof, can comply with building height regulations. When combined with over-large dormers, this solution can ruin the appearance of a house, making it look top-heavy and ridiculous while causing undue weight to bear on the structure below.

Traditionally, Mansard roofs have fewer dormer windows than there are bays below – a practice often ignored by today's over-enthusiastic converters. These dormers should always be placed on the lower slope of the roof, rather than on the more visible higher pitch. They should also be set well back from the parapet wall, and preferably should not be at all visible from the ground below.

ADDING NEW DORMERS

Using the roof space by inserting a dormer window or other opening is always a good way of utilizing empty areas of an old house. However, loft conversions can very easily wreck the visual integrity of a house whose character has been painstakingly built up over centuries.

123

TOP: *Hideous dormers, with wholly unsuitable plastic windows, in Devon.*

BOTTOM: *Recently a number of more sympathetic variants of the rooflight format have come onto the market. Glazing subdivisions and a dark, matt colour are always preferable, and the windows should be as small, and sit as low in the roof, as possible.*

Before beginning any alteration or addition, you clearly need to check whether the roof structure can take the strain of new dormers. This needs to be done by a qualified architect or surveyor who is fully familiar with the method of construction and present-day needs of historic buildings. Secondly, you need to check how planning regulations – particularly listed building laws, if these are appropriate to your home – affect your planned alterations. If new dormers are to be inserted into a listed building, bear in mind that Listed Building Consent, obtained from your local authority planning department, is mandatory, no matter how sympathetic you believe their design to be.

Great care, too, must be taken when designing new dormer windows. Dormers should reflect the style of the building as a whole, and should mirror the size, disposition and spacing of the windows and bays below. This does not mean that they should always be placed directly above a window; traditionally, many dormers were placed between the bays of a facade in order not to over-balance the composition (or, indeed, to cause undue stress on the roof stucture). If a new dormer is to be added to a roof which already includes earlier, historical examples, then use these extant models as your design guide. Surprisingly, this obvious rule of thumb is one which has been frequently ignored over the last forty years.

Dormers should be clad in a material which matches or blends with the rest of the roof. They should also be provided with pitched roofs if this configuration is appropriate for the style and context of the building. They should not, however, project above the top edge of the roof or, in the case of a mansard roof, above the line of the first pitch.

All too often over-large and poorly detailed dormers are inserted into a roof in order to get the maximum possible light into the roofspace, without any consideration of the visual disharmony that can result. Modern dormers can so easily be over-assertive, dominating the facade below and blending poorly with the roof materials and design. If your house has exposed gable ends, sensitively designed small windows in the gables, which match the fenestration of the principal elevations, may prove a good alternative to oversized or over-used dormers.

Obviously the design of dormers sited on front or easily seen elevations needs more careful consideration than one for those placed on hidden rear roofs. However, the fact that the dormer or skylight can rarely be seen should not be an excuse for shoddy design and materials.

INSERTING ROOFLIGHTS

Rooflights or skylights first became popular in the late 18th century, when the top-lighting of staircases, corridors and, later, rooms became all the rage. By the end of the 19th century rooflights were available in a variety of forms, from the unsubtle, single-paned example through multi-light, stained-glass varieties to pantiles actually made of glass.

Where old buildings are involved, dormers are often preferable to skylights, especially on the main elevations. (This stipulation may even be enshrined in local authority policy, as part of the council planning department's local plan.) Skylights can easily ruin the appearance of the whole building if used unwisely, their blank simplicity providing a painful contrast with the aged roof covering and masonry. If used in large numbers, the extensive area of glass that results can totally disrupt the roof both visually and structurally. However, if used sensitively and sympathetically, a simple and reticent, multi-light skylight may prove less of an eyesore in the context of an old building than a poorly designed modern dormer.

If there is no alternative to the installation of skylights, try to ensure that they are hidden by the parapet from street views, or installed on rear or hidden roofs. (Particularly suitable for this purpose are the inner slopes of traditional M-shaped or 'butterfly' roofs.) If on an externally visible roof, they should at least reflect the proportions and disposition of the windows underneath.

The material of the rooflight clearly needs to sympathize with the traditional materials used elsewhere in the house. Stained hardwood or PVC-U plastic rooflights, for example, are simply not acceptable in an old building; not only do these materials look wholly out of place on a traditional roof, but also their life expectancy may prove disappointingly short. At the same time, remember that the rooflight needs to be not only waterproof, but also secure from forced entry. All too often burglars gain access to a house through poorly protected, single-pane rooflights.

Central-pivoting rooflights have now become widespead in Britain's towns and villages. In contrast to earlier, pre-war examples, they are watertight, easy to clean and fairly secure. However, they are still very conspicuous if used in the wrong context on an old roof, and should be confined to comparatively hidden roof slopes and used sparingly. Even if they cannot be seen from the ground, this does not mean that they remain altogether invisible. In hilly areas, for example, single-pane rooflights, punching characterless holes into the traditional roofscape, can often be easily spotted from across the valley. Remember that local authority Listed Building Consent is needed to install a rooflight in any listed building, no matter how obvious or hidden the location.

Rooflights should be kept as regular and unobtrusive as possible, and preferably inserted on inner roof planes – as seen here – rather than on principal elevations.

So-called 'conservation' rooflights are now widely available, made from aluminium or iron and designed to incorporate two or more lights – a format which avoids the blank, featureless look of large areas of plate glass, as well as providing greater security from forced entry. These rooflights also have a low profile, fitting snugly into the roof rather than projecting in unsightly fashion above the upper line of roofing material. This sort of product is always preferable to less sympathetic modern examples; so, if you have to fit a rooflight, shop around first.

DAY-TO-DAY MAINTENANCE

It is important to ensure that gutters are always clear of debris – fallen leaves, live plants, silt, even snow. Clogged valley gutters can cause great damage to the roof structure below. Excess moss, too, should be removed from slates, as moss can harbour damp, and any rain running off a moss- or lichen-covered tile is bound to be more acidic – thus causing erosion below. And, of course, never neglect fallen or slipped slates or tiles: what can take minutes to repair can, if left alone, result in serious long-term damage to your home, which will probably include an outbreak of dry rot. More damage is caused to houses from water penetration than from any other single factor.

As well as making sure that gutters – both obvious and hidden – are clear, it is also useful to keep a watch on the structural health of the parapets.

Ironwork

WROUGHT IRON – the purest form of iron, with a carbon content of less than 1% – was first manufactured around 2000 BC. By about 450 BC it had reached Britain. It was not until the early 15th century, however, that the process of using a blast furnace to smelt iron ore 'pigs' (which were subsequently beaten into wrought iron) was introduced. Blast furnaces originally prospered where iron ore and wood (to make the charcoal needed for smelting) was plentiful; thus by 1700 the heavily wooded area of the Kent–Sussex border had become the centre for British iron production. In 1709, however, Abraham Darby of Coalbrookdale in Shropshire effectively inaugurated the Industrial Revolution by using coke rather than increasingly expensive charcoal to smelt the ore. This not only enabled far higher temperatures to be achieved during the smelting process; it also led to the industry moving nearer the centres of coal production.

During the 17th and 18th centuries highly malleable wrought iron was extensively used for gates, railings and staircases. Cast iron – cast using remelted pig iron, and with a carbon content of up to 5% – was well-known by 1700, but its use was largely confined to the manufacture of coarse, everyday items such as cooking pots, firebacks and cannon balls. It only became widespread following the introduction in 1794 of Wilkinson's efficient 'cupola' blast furnace for remelting pigs.

By 1840 cast iron columns and beams – and cast iron fire-resistant plates – were being inserted into all types of building. Yet, unlike the more fibrous wrought iron, cast iron remained relatively weak and brittle under tension. It was only with the introduction of steel in the later 19th century that a more lasting structural strength could be achieved.

ABOVE: *The development of the bar finial of wrought iron railings, as expounded by Fred Brodnax for The Building of Bath Museum.*

OPPOSITE: *Regency ironwork, including a surviving lampstand, from London's Bloomsbury. The railings would originally have been painted grey or, more likely, dark ('invisible') green.*

RAILINGS AND BALCONIES

Wrought iron railings first appeared in the early 17th century. Cast iron railings were – despite Sir Christopher Wren's vehement opposition – used for the boundary fence around St Paul's Cathedral in 1714; railings were not, however, used to define the perimeter of an urban square until 1735, when they were erected around London's

127

A cast iron baluster of 1785 from the demolished Robert Adam house (latterly the Chinese Embassy) in Portland Place, London, and now in The Brooking Collection.

Lincoln's Inn Fields. Unfortunately, many examples of fine municipal ironwork were removed during World War II, and never returned. (Iron railings were in fact wholly useless to the armaments manufacturers; accordingly, much splendid ironwork rusted away in warehouses for years.)

Early Georgian railings generally comprised heavy, massive uprights terminating in spiked finials in the form of halberds, javelins, arrows or other weapon heads. As the 18th century progressed, railings inevitably became more complex, 'dog-bars' being introduced along the bottom (literally to keep out dogs) and elaborate patterning, often of stamped or cast lead rather than iron, being inserted between the vertical bars. Lead was also used to bed the iron bars into the bare stone.

In 1774 the Adam brothers designed the famous 'heart and honeysuckle' railings for 7 Adam Street, part of their ill-fated Adelphi development. The Neoclassically inspired anthemion (honeysuckle) motif and urn finials influenced countless designs in the newly fashionable streets of towns such as Brighton, Cheltenham and Philadelphia. By 1780, too, iron balconies or 'verandahs', which projected further than the familiar iron window-guards, were becoming increasingly common. Cantilevered out from the first floor, they were generally painted green (not black or white, which are modern conceptions), and were supported not only by the brackets visible on their undersides but also by iron beams which extended far into the house.

STRUCTURAL IRONWORK

In 1778 Darby and Pritchard erected the first iron bridge in the world at Coalbrookdale in Shropshire. This was rapidly followed by other iron bridges such as Thomas Telford's Pont Cysyllte Aqueduct of 1795, which employed cast iron arches spanning 45 feet. In 1815 the architect John Nash (whose first iron bridge – erected at Stanford Court, Worcestershire in 1795 – had instantly collapsed) installed the celebrated 'bamboo staircase' at Brighton Pavilion; not only were the balusters (cast and painted to imitate bamboo) of iron, but also the stair treads, risers and even the handrail. Iron framing was also used for many of the rooms in the remodelled Pavilion – so much so that by the mid-1820s Nash was (with considerable exaggeration) declaring himself to be 'the principal user, and perhaps I may add the introducer of cast-iron in the construction of buildings'.

From the 1780s onwards even windows were being constructed in iron – although the glazing bars or muntins could be of brass, copper or even bronze. This advance enabled glazing bar thicknesses to be reduced at no cost to the overall integrity and stability of the structure.

IRON CONSERVATORIES

In 1815 one Sir George Mackenzie published an article which called for the introduction of a glass greenhouse whose roof would be 'parallel to the vaulted surface of the heavens, or to the plane of the sun's orbit', and which included a revolutionary design for a greenhouse built not as the usual, straight-sided box but as a half-dome. The following year the architectural and gardening writer J.C. Loudon patented the curved cast iron glazing bar, for specific use in conservatories. No longer did plant-houses have to be flat-roofed boxes; new, curved-roof conservatories presented a far larger area for the sun to shine through, and were thus far more effective at plant propagation. In 1823 Loudon erected a domed conservatory on the side of his own home in Bayswater's Porchester Terrace, and was soon enthusing about its advantages:

> The greenhouse may be designed in any form, and placed in almost any situation . . .
> Even a house looking due north, if glazed on three sides of the roof, will preserve plants
> in a healthy, vigorous state. The curvilinear principle applied to this class of structures
> admits of every combination of form . . . and soon, the clumsy shed-like wooden or
> mixed roofs now in use will be erected only in nursery and market gardens.

Metal-framed glasshouses were soon provided with another new invention: steam heating supplied through cast iron piping, first attempted in 1788 and widespread by 1820.

MAINTENANCE AND REPAIR

Decorative ironwork is often not as decayed as it may seem. Rust (oxidized iron) can occupy more than seven times the area of unoxidized ironwork; thus, when the rust has been cleaned away, the problem may not be as serious as it originally appeared.

Basic rules to follow in repairing ironwork are to retain as much of the original metal as possible – i.e. to repair rather than to replace; to replace like with like (for example, replacing wrought iron with wrought iron, and not with cast iron); and to use tried and trusted traditional repair techniques wherever possible. Remove all dirt, rust, paint and grease before repainting. And do not be afraid of rust; underneath the oxidization there may well be enough unoxidized metal to form the basis of a viable repair.

The prime function of paint on ironwork is as a protective layer, not to provide decoration. Thus paint must be applied all over in order to be effective. If removing paint prior to repair, remember that you are thereby eradicating the ironwork's paint history, making it impossible to determine the original colourings in the future; it is always helpful to leave at least one, small area unstripped.

The early (1820s) curvilinear conservatory at Grove House in London's Regent Park.

129

Mouldings

A SOUND KNOWLEDGE OF the forms and correct use of mouldings was considered essential for any Georgian or Victorian designer. As Stephen Riou pointed out in his manual *The Grecian Orders of Architecture* in 1768, 'Since mouldings do, as it were, compose the alphabet of architecture', one needed 'a perfect knowledge of their several attributions and combinations, . . . their uses and shapes'.

Mouldings originated in the 17th century as wooden fittings. These were used not as decorative pieces inserted into the completed shell of a building, as they are today; instead they were employed to decorate integral structural features that were exposed to view (ceiling beams, door and fireplace surrounds, newel staircases and so on) or simply to cover a structural joint or an unsightly transition between different planes – allowing the parts beneath to settle and move, as well as providing a more visually cohesive display of light and shadow. By definition, these structural mouldings were heavily three-dimensional; this quality remained characteristic of mouldings for some time after they ceased to have a structural function and were merely nailed on or 'applied'. Mouldings were also used on the exterior of the house; moulded architraves, for example, helped to shed rainwater from vulnerable doors and windows.

In many cases mouldings were carefully placed to correspond to the vertical intervals of the Classical column; thus the skirting (known in America as the baseboard) corresponded to the base, the dado to the pedestal and the cornice to the entablature. This architectural allegory held true throughout the Georgian era and beyond.

The earliest type of applied mouldings in common use were the box cornice and 'bolection' moulding linking two adjoining planes, or covering a structural joint. These early mouldings were necessarily heavy and substantial. However, as the 18th century progressed, architects were increasingly concerned to conceal all of the real structural elements of a building; accordingly, mouldings became flatter and less pronounced, and surface decoration took the place of depth. As the structural function of mouldings waned, so did the necessity of making them from solid wood. Thus architects

OPPOSITE: *Simple, early Georgian panelling, comprising little more than stiles and rails with elementary cornices, dado rails and skirtings. In the Georgian period pine panelling such as this – and indeed the front door – would have always been painted, for protection as well as for decoration.*

131

Typical surround mouldings from Georgian Bath. 1: a cornice, comprising large and small ogees and a fillet; 2: an architrave, incorporating two ogees and a bead; 3: an architrave, comprising an ovolo and a bead; 4: another architrave, comprising a cavetto, a fillet and a bead.

and builders began to turn to a cheaper, lighter and more easily cast material: plaster. By 1720 both wooden and plaster mouldings were in widespread use.

Early Georgian mouldings, derived directly from the forms of Ancient Rome and Renaissance Italy, were large and robust – none more so than the egg-and-dart motifs which so characterize the Palladian interiors of the 1720s, 30s and 40s. In contrast to the practice of the preceding century, they were invariably painted, resulting in a less heavy and more refined effect. (This desired finish is, sadly, often ruined today by the modern fashion for indiscriminate stripping of old woodwork.)

By the middle of the 18th century the practice of installing wooden panelling above dado level had become rather unfashionable; the trend was increasingly to leave the wall above the chair rail of flat plaster, and to cover this with paint or wallpaper. (In 1756 the architect Isaac Ware noted sadly that 'Paper has, in a great measure, taken the place of sculpture [i.e. wood or plaster mouldings] and the hand of art is banished from a part of the house in which it used to display itself very happily.') By 1770 the pattern-book authors were beginning to argue in print over the respective merits of the new, subtler and more archaeologically correct, Neoclassical mouldings being introduced by Robert Adam, James Stuart and their fellow-Grecians. Whereas Early Georgian plaster mouldings projected boldly into the room, the new 'Greek' forms were of lower relief and more modest profile. Thus while the Palladian ovolo moulding, for example, was an exact quarter-circle in cross-section, the profile of its Greek equivalent was flatter and segmental, being only a part of this quarter-circle.

By the end of the 18th century plaster mouldings were light, graceful and of increasingly low relief. 'Grecian' decorative motifs were very popular – particularly the anthemion, the palmette and the Vitruvian scroll. More typical of the restraint and simplicity of Regency plasterwork, however, was the most common moulding of the period: the humble bead. When used in a linked combination of two or more beads (the outermost edges of which were usually flush with the adjacent fillet or surface), the moulding was termed 'reeding'. Reeding was applied to cornices, chimneypieces, door surrounds, dados and skirting; there were even 'reeded' glazing bars, set with two or three deeply undercut ('quirked') beads. Quirking was a Greek device, used to obtain a greater sense of depth and play of shadows from a basically low-relief moulding or surface, which was very prevalent during the first half of the 19th century. Deeply quirked, single beads were often found placed between wall panels or employed to frame niches or to emphasize arches.

By 1820 plaster mouldings were generally far less obtrusive than their 18th-century predecessors. Certainly the more daring and innovative interiors of Britain's grand mansions – or indeed of the homes of architects such as Hope or Soane – included designs and motifs that were heavily influenced by the latest developments in France or Germany, or by the latest discoveries in Italy or Greece. However, the design of more modestly sized Regency walls and ceilings tended to follow Rudolf Ackermann's sensible advice that a 'simple and chaste character is best'. At the same time, the interest in academic Neoclassicism, which expressed itself in the revivals of the Greek and Egyptian styles, brought a renewed emphasis on solidity and weight. One effect of this seems to have been the popularity of the reeded moulding, often used with paterae (small square panels) at the corners – a form frequently found on Regency chimneypieces, cornices and architraves.

The Georgian period was the golden age of the applied moulding. In Victorian Britain the design and siting of mouldings became less influenced by academic considerations, as their Classical origins were forgotten or deliberately ignored. The results were sometimes quite crude or even rather bizarre, and many Victorian mouldings bear little resemblance to their supposed Georgian antecedents.

Chunky egg-and-dart cornice moulding of the 1770s from Annapolis, Maryland.

Early Georgian panelling, together with an appropriately simple fire surround, in a first floor drawing room in London's Spitalfields.

RESTORING MOULDINGS

The new owner of an old house may be faced with the task of restoring the character of a building that has lost many of its mouldings – perhaps as a result of conversion, of neglect or of a viciously inappropriate modernization. Where they have been removed, their careful reinstatement can dramatically enhance a plain room.

In all cases, the work should be approached cautiously, and a minute examination of the room should be made before beginning. Dados and skirtings long since removed may have their profiles sharply preserved in the built-up layers of paint on a door architrave; their positions may show as ghostings against the wall plaster when the wallcoverings are removed. Panelled doors and balustrades are often found excellently preserved between modern layers of painted hardboard.

If the house is in a uniform terrace, it is always worth inspecting your neighbour's house in case it has any mouldings which have been lost from your own. It is not difficult to draw out their profiles using a ruler, set square and commercially available profile gauge, and any competent wood-machinist will be able to duplicate them for you. Wherever possible, avoid off-the-peg mouldings, since for anything beyond the most basic skirtings and architraves they tend to be historically inaccurate and fairly crude.

The complexity of mouldings is proportional to the pretention of the room; the humbler the function (and indeed the fewer the visitors), the more modest the mouldings. Thus, while drawing rooms on the ground or first floors may feature elaborate cornices and rich, heavy doorcases, rooms at the top of the house may possess only simple box cornices, a rudimentary dado and perhaps no skirting mouldings at all. If reintroducing period mouldings of plaster or wood into a house which has lost all trace of the original pattern, it is very important to keep this context firmly in mind. Wooden mouldings and panelling bought wholesale from architectural salvage outlets, for example, are often re-used in unsuitable and incongruous settings. Over-sized and over-elaborate mouldings set in a small, modest room inevitably look cramped and ridiculous. Remember that what looks splendid in a grand country house – or a cavernous warehouse – may be quite inappropriate for an ordinary terraced home.

Georgian farmhouses and cottages can raise different problems. The simplest cottages have boarded doors and often originally had no skirtings or architraves at all. These latter features were often added by the Victorians, and good examples should be retained.

As a general rule, mouldings should not be used to change the character of a house; they should rather be used with restraint, to draw out the character that is already there.

MOULDING TYPES

The vocabulary of Classical mouldings is voluminous, and the multiplicity of terms often extremely confusing. However, as Dan Cruickshank has pointed out, 'all moulded decorations are based upon two simple and complementary forms: the curved convex quadrant called the ovolo (also occasionally called the echinus) and the flat-faced right-angular fillet' (*Life in the Georgian City* (1990), 167). The basic varieties of mouldings are best explained visually, as in the diagram opposite.

USING PATTERN-BOOKS

For those seeking to repair or re-create Georgian mouldings, perhaps the most important part of this guide is the Further Reading section (see page 234), with its list of suggested pattern-books and modern sources. However, remember that, while these Georgian publications may serve as a useful pictorial reference, the mouldings that they demonstrate are by no means suitable for every location in the house, nor do they represent every possible permutation of the Classical vocabulary.

Different types of decorative mouldings in common use.

Astragal
A small convex moulding, often decorated with a bead and reel low relief pattern.

Bead
A small cylindrical moulding, often enriched with ornament resembling a string of beads.

Bolection
A moulding used to cover the joint between two members with different surface levels. It projects beyond both surfaces. Frequently used in 17th and early 18th C joinery.

Cavetto
A concave moulding whose profile is usually a quarter of a circle.

Cyma recta
The cyma is a moulding consisting of a double curve. The cyma recta or ogee moulding is concave above and convex below.

Cyma reversa
The cyma reversa, or reverse ogee, also called a keel moulding, is convex above and concave below.

Fillet
A narrow flat band used to separate two mouldings, or to terminate a series of mouldings as in a cornice, sometimes called a listel.

Ovolo
A convex moulding, usually a quarter of a circle, sometimes ornamented with egg and dart or similar motifs.

Quirk
An acute V-shaped groove, often found between a convex moulding and a flat member. Also used to afford shadow to an ogee or ovolo.

Reeding
A form of surface decoration, consisting of parallel convex mouldings

Scotia
A small concave moulding between the two tori in the base of a column. It throws a deep shadow.

Torus
(plural: tori) A bold convex moulding used in the bases of columns.

15

Floors

THROUGHOUT THE GEORGIAN PERIOD oak was considered the best material for good timber floors. However, in practice most households had to make do with inferior woods, which were usually partly or wholly covered to hide their raw, knotty surfaces. Deal – squared boards of pine or fir from the Baltic or, later, from North America – was particularly prevalent from the early 18th century onwards in Britain and on the east coast of America, where the scarcity, and expense, of both English oak and marble resulted in nearly all Colonial floors being made entirely from deal.

Until the end of the Georgian era there were no particular rules as to the dimensions of floorboards; nor were the boards necessarily of a consistent size within a single floor. Patent machines to plane timber uniformly were introduced during the 1790s, but it was not until the 1830s that identical boards were produced by steam-powered, mechanical saws. The popularity of fitted carpets made the elaborately designed wooden floor less of a necessity – a development noted by Sheraton, who remarked that 'since the introduction of carpets, fitted all over the floor of a room, the nicety of flooring anciently practised in the best houses, is now laid aside.'

By the early 1700s the inhabitants of New England, where white pine (though not oak) was initially plentiful, were using wide floorboards of between one and two feet in width. By the end of the 18th century, however, they were forced to use narrower boards of yellow pine, and by 1830 New England households were being provided with floors of deal planks only four to six inches in width.

The best – and most expensive – way of fixing floorboards was to have them linked by means of horizontal dowels, then face-nailed to the joists below. More usually, however, boards were simply nailed at their edges, at an angle of 45 degrees, and the joint subsequently concealed by the next board. In 1803 Sheraton noted:

> There are three methods by which floors are laid. First, with plain jointed edges, and nailed down. Second, jointing and ploughing the edges to receive a wainscot tongue about an inch broad, and a bare quarter thick. . . . Third, when they are laid with douwells of oak-board into the edge.

OPPOSITE: Robert Adam's floor design of 1767 for the entrance hall at Osterley Park, Middlesex. The materials are relatively modest: Portland stone interset with slate.

139

Not long after this account appeared, metal plates, rather than dowel, began to be inserted into the grooving in adjacent boards, to ensure an even firmer joint. And by 1833 Loudon was recommending thicker boards – 'sometimes . . . three inches thick' – to give added strength and 'to lessen the risk of their being burnt through by fire'.

Throughout the 18th century single-joisted floors (with the joists all running in the same direction), supported by large structural timbers, were still very much the rule for the average house. In terrace housing of the period the joists ran from front to back or from side to side, bearing on the external and (if they existed) party walls, and possibly on the central, structural spine wall too. This simple method of construction allowed the large, structural beams to spread the weight of the spine wall, with its doors, door-cases and stairs, to the outer shell. If there were greater loading requirements, or the house was larger and the floor necessarily more complex, then additional, transverse joists and beams could be added. This was not always done, though, with any precise knowledge of the effect it would have; it was only in 1840 that the first guide to gauging joist thicknesses for specific spans was published. However, the upper floors of most later Georgian houses did not need to bear enormous weights, as most entertaining was done on the ground floor and not the first, as had often been the case earlier in the Georgian era. The concept of the 'rustic' ground floor of services and servant accommodation, with incoming guests proceeding directly to the principal rooms on the floor above, was by 1800 somewhat outdated in all but the grandest homes.

Georgian or colonial timber floors, in common with grander examples of stone or marble, were often limewashed. This valuable protective coating is still widely available, and allows floors and walls to 'breathe' – that is, permits moisture to pass in and out of the underlying material rather than causing it to be trapped inside, prompting damp problems. The visual effect of limewashing wooden boards was to produce an attractive silvery sheen, of the type modern 'limed' furniture tries (but sadly often fails) to recapture. In 1772 an American visitor noted that English deal floors 'are washed and rubbed almost daily' with lime water, resulting in 'a whitish appearance, and an air of freshness and cleanliness'.

Diagrams of possible arrangements of floor joists from one of the most useful of Regency builders' manuals: Peter Nicholson's Mechanical Exercises *of 1812.*

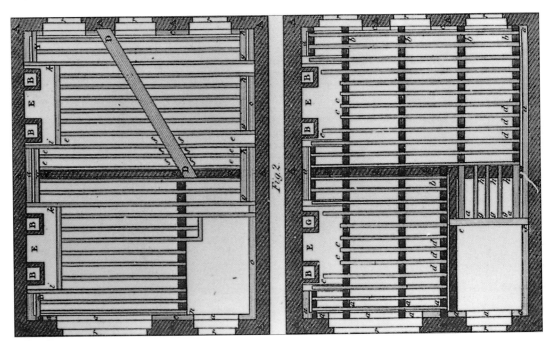

This pine floor – at the Carlyle House, Alexandria, Virginia – has been covered with a reproduction floorcloth of the type common during the Georgian period. However, painted designs similar to this (especially patterns which mimicked tessellated marble or stone) were also popular.

A similar white patina was achieved through the widespread practice of cleaning wooden floors by scrubbing them with dry sand, sometimes mixed with fresh herbs. Alternatively, aromatic herbs such as mint or tansy could be rubbed into the grain to give the boards both a fresh odour and a slightly darker stain. Georgian floors were *never* varnished.

If the floorboards were not made of seasoned oak or other expensive wood, they were always covered in some fashion. The painting of floorboards in oil paint was very common, especially in areas such as New England where wooden floors were universal. In the early 19th century Thomas Jefferson was painting the floorboards of the entrance hall at Monticello a solid green; however, as with clay or plaster floors, wooden boards were frequently painted to resemble a grander floor finish, most often with a pattern suggesting marble blocks. A terracotta paint finish, often superimposed with a yellow glaze or with limewash, was also widely used – a covering obviously designed to recall the traditional (and yet very modest) clay floor. And there were countless other variants, involving soot and chalk as well as oil paints. By 1830 wooden floors in America were being regularly painted in brightly coloured stripes, with a different colour for each board.

By the 1800s the stencilling of floorboards, long popular in the United States but previously never very fashionable in Britain, was also enjoying a vogue, while parquetry was back in fashion for the first time since the early 18th century, used not for whole floors, but merely for the newly fashionable borders, of between one and two feet in width, which were now left around the carpet edges. This in turn prompted a whole-sale revival of parquetry, at least in the larger homes, by the end of the period. In 1837 – the year in which Victoria ascended the British throne – Peter Nicholson was writing that 'the fashion for laying floors with various coloured woods, disposed in patterns, seems now to become more general in this country.'

York stone flags from a kitchen floor in north London.

CLAY FLOORS

Floors varied in direct proportion to the household's wealth and pretension. More basic homes, especially in rural areas, were generally provided with 'stuccoed' or clay floors. The 'stucco' floors of cottages and outbuildings were made from a basic plaster recipe, which usually included a natural pigment – most often pig's blood – to give the dried 'stucco' a brown colour. In common with so many surfaces of the Georgian era, these floors were often disguised as something else: painted to resemble black and white marble squares, or simply covered with a layer of whitewash or limewash. In 1814 P.F. Tingry's *Painter's and Varnisher's Guide* noted that:

> Some floors have been executed of plaster, on which the lemon yellow colour destined for *parquets* of oak produces a very good effect.

Alas, clay or stucco floors rarely survive: either the surfaces broke up through constant wear, or social aspirations prompted their replacement by more sophisticated wood or stone alternatives. It is interesting to note that, at the other end of the social scale, floors made of scagliola, a plaster compound cast and polished to look like marble, were also denoted by the name 'stucco'. The vast amounts of money laid out on these rare and colourful objects, however, were usually wasted: ironically, scagliola floors proved even more fragile than their distant, humbler cousins.

SOLID FLOORS

For those who could afford it – or for those who lived near a suitable quarry – solid floors represented the height of Georgian taste. The classic solid floor comprised large slabs of Portland or similarly pale-coloured stone interset with small diamonds of dark grey slate or marble, or perhaps variations on the theme of black and white marble squares. This type of heavy flooring was most prevalent in ground floor hallways, both to impress visitors and to bear the constant weight of social assemblies.

For the poorer households, random flags or tessellated brick paviours, reddened with pigments based on animal blood, had to suffice. Loudon's *Encyclopaedia* of 1833 featured thirteen different designs for paving in coloured bricks. Coloured tiles, however, were more of a Victorian fashion. Although they were occasionally used in the grander hallways of the 1830s, the mass-production of sophisticated, hard-wearing tiles, often with indented patterns filled with slip, only truly began in the 1840s.

REPAIRING FLOORS

Old timber floors rarely have to be replaced completely – whatever your builder may say. Repairs that are both structurally sound and visually satisfactory are easy to achieve with a little care and attention. Repairs to floorboards, and to timber floor construction in general, are expertly and clearly dealt with in the SPAB's concise technical pamphlets (see Further Reading, page 234).

Scrubbed wooden floorboards in General Washington's bedchamber at Mount Vernon. Scrubbing with limewater or sand would help to give even plain deal boards a silvery sheen.

CLEANING FLOORS

Exposed wooden floors were often waxed and polished during the Georgian period; they were also occasionally stained brown to imitate finer woods. They were cleaned using fresh flowers and herbs, or with dry- or wet-rubbed sand or fuller's earth. When cleaning boards today, ensure that as little water as possible is used, otherwise damp or warping problems may result.

Stains can be removed from wooden or solid floors in a variety of ways. What follows is a quick summary of some of the most common – and the most sympathetic. When tackling stains, always choose the gentlest method first; this way you will avoid unduly disfiguring the flooring material.

Grease   Traditionally removed from wooden floors using poultices of clay or fuller's earth. Today repeated poulticing is still the best way of removing unsightly stains from wooden floors, although acetone, white spirit or even lemon juice will remove simple stains from stone floors. Poultices, which draw the moisture – and the stain with it – from the stone or wood as they dry out, can be made from fuller's earth, talc, powdered chalk or even shredded paper towels. It is important to wet the floor before applying them. Gentle poultices can be applied using a simple solution of starch and hot water.

Salt   Stone or marble floors, if over-soaked, can be damaged through salt migrating to the surface. Avoid excess washing in removing these salt stains: a damp mop will do, or if this fails, a general purpose chemical cleaner.

Organic Stains   Use household ammonia or a 2% solution of hydrogen peroxide. As with all such treatments, always rinse the area with clean water afterwards.

Rubber Marks   Apply sparingly a solution of equal parts of water and white spirit, with a drop of washing-up liquid.

Chewing Gum   Freeze the offending mess using ice cubes, then chip away when it has become sufficiently brittle. Proprietary aerosol products which freeze their targets rapidly are available commercially.

Old Paint   Water-based paints can be treated with simple cold water – used with restraint. Emulsions can be removed with white or methylated spirits, although old gloss paint may require the use of a chemical solvent.

Cement   Use a very weak solution of hydrochloric acid, or a proprietary cleaner.

General Stains (Wood Floors)   A solution of glycerine and water may help to loosen the stain. Steel wool can be used for more stubborn timber floor stains; if this fails, try using a specialized wood bleach – although this may have the effect of discolouring the wood too.

General Stains (Solid Floors)   Cleaning marble floors with a very weak solution of ammonia will remove all but the most stubborn stains – which may need poulticing. Never use abrasive cleaners, or sanders or grinders, on good quality solid floors. And never use ammonia with bleach: the result will be a toxic gas.

MODERN FLOOR FINISHES

Old floorboards should never be sanded. As Philip Hughes has pointed out, 'If a board has suffered at all from beetle attack sanding will remove the smooth surface of the board and leave a ragged mess of worm-ridden timber beneath.'

Sealants are all too often both unsightly and inappropriate. Polyurethane and epoxy resin coatings, for example, are very difficult to remove, tend to yellow, and can scratch and chip easily. Other chemical sealants may need constant maintenance and replacement, causing damage to the floor itself in the process, while most sealants tend to 'track' (the condition where a distinct path is worn down in the floor surface) with constant use.

Proprietary floor sealers are always to be preferred to polyurethane varnishes. Often the most suitable sealant, however, is the one which is the most natural. Boiled linseed oil, for example, is considered by many to be the most appropriate sealant for ceramic floors, while conservators' waxes are probably the best material to use on wooden floors. Whatever the flooring material, before you attempt to seal always seek independent advice, and, having received this, always experiment first on a small, inconspicuous area.

If you decide to insulate your timber floor, make sure that there is proper ventilation below the boards. Without a free passage of air, moisture can become trapped in the timber, causing severe damp problems.

Most modern varnishes and 'enhancing' wood finishes produce an unsympathetic and decidedly ahistorical result if used on old timber floors. Linseed oil should also be avoided, as it tends to attract the dirt and to darken with age. In general, if you have an oak floor, it is best to leave the material to speak for itself. If, on the other hand, your timber floor is of deal (cut fir planks) or pine, remember that the Georgians rarely left such floors uncovered, using carpets, floorcloths or painted decoration to hide the inferior and often unsightly grain.

However you decide to cover your floor, don't forget to consider it in the context of the rest of the room; so often today floors are allowed to dominate, rather than to complement, old interiors.

Tessellated marble floor designs from John Carwitham's Various Kinds of Floor Decorations . . . for Ornamenting the Floors of Halls, Rooms, Summer Houses, etc. *of 1739.*

145

Staircases

16

BY 1700 THE STAIRCASE was possibly the most impressive architectural feature of a well-to-do middle- or upper-class home. Of 'closed string' or 'open string' design (i.e. with the tread ends hidden by a rising architrave or left showing) the Early Georgian staircase comprised handsome wood balusters supporting a sturdy handrail. If the wood was expensive – say fine oak or West Indian mahogany – then it would have been coated only with layers of beeswax. Most homes, however, could only afford a pine staircase (although perhaps one provided with a handrail of higher-quality wood), and this was invariably painted.

Early 18th-century balusters generally comprised a Doric column resting upon an urn, the column being short and stubby and separated from the urn by one or two squared blocks or 'tablets'. As the century progressed, the columns became longer and more slender; moreover, not only could they be straight-sided, but, alternatively, they could be twisted by a proficient wood-turner. Twisted balusters could be used on their own, or alternated with straight-sided ones; a popular arrangement was to have three balusters on each tread, with the middle one differing in treatment from its neighbours. Sometimes, too, the tablet between the column and urn was omitted, creating a more graceful, vertically oriented effect. Rarely, though, were wooden balusters shaped wholly in the form of uninterrupted Classical columns.

Handrails tended to be of a superior wood to the balusters, and were often 'ramped' – bent sharply upwards in a swooping curve – to take account of the changes of level at the various landings. At the bottom of the staircase the handrail terminated in a newel post. Newel posts, even in the Early Georgian period, were seldom allowed to project above the handrail; in later Georgian houses they were dispensed with altogether – although for reasons of practicality they remained in use for tortuous servants' stairs.

To complement the fine carving or turning of the handrail and balusters, open string staircases were often provided with fine, delicately carved tread ends. These were often splendidly detailed – principally so as to be admired by passers-by in the hallway – and should be retained wherever they survive.

ABOVE: *A detail from the principal staircase at the Powel House, Philadelphia. This stair was constructed in 1765 of red mahogany from the Caribbean island of Santo Domingo. The button at the top of the newel post can be removed to reveal a hiding place for documents.*

OPPOSITE: *An impressive mid-Georgian oak staircase from Myles Place, Salisbury. The balusters, grouped three to a tread, have tall pedestals corresponding with the height of the following riser.*

147

A typical staircase of the 1730s in a north London house. As was the rule, at the second floor landing – beyond which only children, tenants or servants would go – the turned balusters and carved handrail metamorphose into straight sticks with a plain rail.

Most stairs were generally well lit by Georgian standards, either by side windows or by top-lighting provided by a skylight – a solution that became increasingly popular towards the end of the 18th century. Often, however, the complex design of the staircase inside the house meant that the windows required to light it did not correspond with the formal Palladian proportions of the exterior. In this case, it was the staircase that was required to give way – stair treads or whole landings often cutting inexplicably across the middle of windows in order to preserve the calm repose of a Georgian facade.

The social hierarchy of the house – with poorer servants, lodgers or whole families in the upper storeys, away from the principal sources of heat and water – was reflected in the design of the stair. The higher you ascended, the plainer the staircase became, with twisted balusters replaced by straight-sided examples, or the latter by plain, unadorned sticks. Plain sticks, of either circular or square sections, also featured in the secondary, servants' staircase, which was, unsurprisingly, rarely provided with the type of expensive elaboration afforded to the principal stair.

In the most fashionable homes of the 1750s sturdy turned balusters were sometimes replaced with so-called 'Chinese' fretwork, to produce the remarkably modern effect now generally known by the term 'Chinese Chippendale'. Such fancies, however, rarely journeyed further than the pages of Chippendale, Langley or the Halfpennys.

By the 1770s, efforts to conceal the basic structure of the staircase were reflected in an increasing slenderness of the balusters and less emphasis on newel posts. And

Detail of turned stair balusters of the 1740s from The Brooking Collection. The Collection, comprising countless architectural items rescued from old buildings about to be, or in the process of being, demolished, is now partly housed at Greenwich University's Dartford, Kent campus.

149

RIGHT: *Twisted, 'barley-sugar' balusters supporting an oak-grained handrail in a Spitalfields house of the mid-1720s.*

OPPOSITE: *Robert Adam's revolutionary staircase at Osterley Park (c. 1770), in which slender, blue-painted, cast iron balusters carry a thin mahogany handrail, carved with Vitruvian scroll ornament. While the main supports are of iron, many of the balusters' decorative elements are of cast brass or lead.*

150

This fretwork staircase, of a style often known today as 'Chinese Chippendale', may look modern, but in fact dates from the 1750s. What is modern, however, is the coat of brilliant white paint. The original colour would possibly have been of stone or wood, or perhaps a green.

turned wooden balusters were distinctly out of fashion in metropolitan areas by the last decades of the 18th century, having been replaced by thin, square-section 'stick' balusters. By the 1780s, too, iron balusters were beginning to appear.

In 1745 two important works on staircase design appeared. Abraham Swan's *The British Architect, or the Builder's Treasury of Staircases* featured countless variants of the traditional wooden stair, complete with profiles and measurements for the constituent parts. More innovatory, though, was W. and J. Welldon's *The Smith's Right Hand*, which represented the first original collection of British designs for wrought ironwork of all kinds – including wrought iron balusters. This was a bold step: to replace the turned or twisted wooden baluster with a metal object at once stronger and more graceful. During the next thirty years, however, the Gothic, Chinese and Rococo scrollwork that featured so prominently in the Welldons' manual gave way to more rigid and rectilinear (and therefore more easily constructed) Neoclassical balusters, inevitably incorporating typically Neoclassical motifs such as the anthemion, the palmette or the lyre.

By 1800, indeed, cast or wrought iron balusters had become increasingly common. Often merely the mahogany, oak or grained pine handrail remained as a reminder of the traditional wooden stair. Even the treads and risers could be of iron, while in place of the bulky, wooden newel posts of the 18th century came sinuous, S-shaped terminations of thin, iron balusters or sticks. Some designers dispensed with the soffits under the stairs altogether, creating the impression of an open string staircase that appeared to be made merely of treads and risers piled up on top of each other in mid-air. By the 1820s the most radically planned houses were not even bothering to hide the ingenious iron supports. At Sezincote in Gloucestershire, for example, the iron girders which carried the main stair out were left totally bare, and pierced in a decorative fashion.

From the mid-18th century onwards British staircases were invariably covered with some type of utilitarian carpet or drugget (see chapter 22). This sort of luxury was a source of amazement to foreign visitors. In the 1780s, for example, the French traveller La Rochefoucauld observed not only that the drawing room was 'reached by a spotlessly clean staircase' (of which the handrail was usually 'of mahognay in beautiful condition'), but that 'you are upon mats and carpets everywhere' and that 'there is always a strip of drugget on the stairs'. His contemporary, the Prussian von Archenholz, went even further, recording that in English houses 'the staircase . . . is covered with the richest carpets'. The richness of such coverings helped to emphasize the importance of the staircase to British and colonial households.

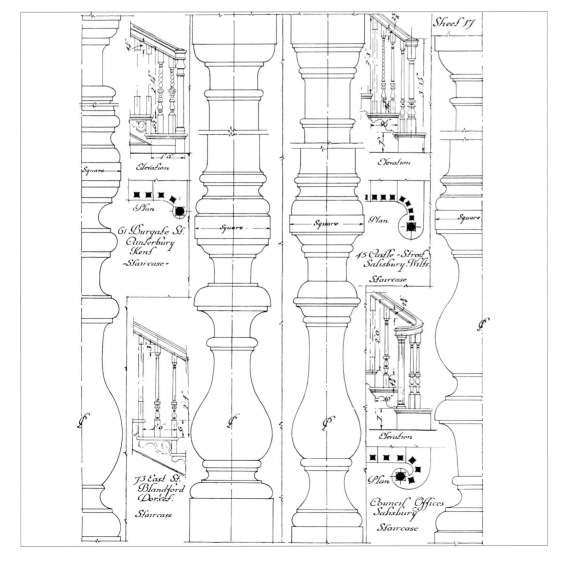

Early Georgian staircase designs from Canterbury, Blandford Forum and Salisbury, as interpreted by Tunstall Small and Christopher Woodbridge in their inter-war pattern-book Architectural Turned Woodwork of the 16th, 17th and 18th Centuries.

17

Fireplaces

THE BASIC DISPOSITION of the chimneypiece remained roughly the same from the mid-17th century until after World War II: a projecting lintel-entablature supported by columns, pilasters or consoles which, from the 1660s onwards, generally carried a large overmantel. Until the early 18th century chimneypieces remained very plain and were rarely decorated; it was only with the new Palladian designers of the 1720s that profuse decoration became the norm for chimneypieces in important rooms. Many of these Palladian chimneypieces of the 1720s, 30s and 40s were heavily ornate, with ponderous swags and scrolls and large shells and masks in the style of Inigo Jones and his Palladian disciple William Kent. They were frequently taken from the new architectural pattern-books which were now available to any architect, sculptor, mason or even houseowner. By the late 1740s lighter, more indisciplined Rococo designs had begun to appear; however, even these were tame in comparison with their French models, and most houseowners continued to employ the stock Palladian styles with which they were most comfortable and familiar.

William Chambers' *Treatise on Civil Architecture* of 1759 laid down the basic rules for the proportion of chimneypieces. 'The size of the chimney', he declared, 'must depend on the dimensions of the room wherein it is placed' (sound advice often ignored today). Similarly, while chimneypieces could be constructed from a wide variety of materials ('stone, marble, or . . . a mixture of these, with wood, scagliola, ormoulu or some other unfragile substances'), in decorating them 'regard must be had to the nature of the place where they are to be employed.' Chambers' advice was both practical and aesthetic. Recommending that fireplaces should not be placed on an outside wall, since the unsupported stacks above would be more liable to collapse, he also advanced the somewhat prudish precept that 'all nudities and indecent representations must be avoided, both in chimneypieces and in every other ornament of apartments to which children, ladies, and other modest, grave persons, have constant recourse.'

OPPOSITE: *A painted pine fire surround of the 1730s from a second floor room in Stoke Newington, north London. Only during the 19th century did the conceit of installing pretentious projecting chimneypieces even in the more modest rooms really begin to take hold.*

155

Under the influence of Chambers' great rival Robert Adam, chimneypieces became less heavy in design, and the ponderous, high-relief Palladian decoration was replaced with low-relief, small scale motifs of Neoclassical origin – particularly urns, delicate swags and figures from Classical mythology. By 1790 the transformation was complete, the Regency chimneypiece being both simpler and more reticent than its Palladian predecessors. Indeed as a key feature in the room it was often excessively plain, with little or no superimposed decoration. Frequently it was only the two small paterae inserted at the top corners of the surround, or recessed reeding at the sides, which relieved the overall severity of design; even the central tablet, the focus for applied decoration earlier in the century, was generally left unadorned.

Architectural elements, and not surface decoration, were now accorded the prime role in the composition. Outside the homes of the richest families (who could possibly afford the latest French confection) Regency chimneypieces rarely varied from this standard, rectilinear form; supporting pilasters were now rarely tapered, and attendant caryatids or terms were devices which only guarded the fires of the wealthy. With the Gothic revival of the 1820s, however, decorative licence was back in fashion. The Gothic designs featured in Rudolf Ackermann's influential *Repository of the Arts* were covered with low-relief but vigorous embellishments, usually based on those ubiquitous motifs, the quatrefoil and the crocket.

The design of Late Georgian fireplaces was profoundly affected by technological improvements. For the most part, 17th- and 18th-century examples had been too large to function efficiently. The invention of the Rumford grate in 1796 (see page 161) engendered a revolution in attitudes to the arrangement of the fireplace, as householders saw the need for more precisely controlled grates and for smaller fireplace

Even the grandest homes often boasted surprisingly reticent chimney surrounds. This coolly rectilinear chimneypiece design of 1794 by Henry Holland was devised for the Prince of Wales' sumptuous London residence of Carlton House.

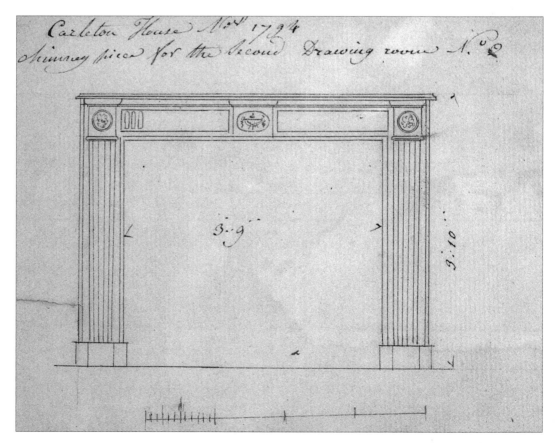

English Delftware fireplace tiles of the mid-18th century. From Hans van Lemmen's Delftware Tiles *(Shire, 1986).*

openings. Thus the Regency fireplace grew not only increasingly simple, but also increasingly small. Paradoxically, though, the fireplace was more than ever the focus of the room. From the 1780s onwards furniture began to be moved more informally around the principal rooms and, given the vagaries of the British climate, it naturally gravitated towards the fire. Ackermann held that the resultant, heightened prominence of the fireplace in the principal rooms of the house was a peculiarly British solution; the corresponding effect, he asserted, was a healthier household and a healthier nation, with the fireplace 'the rallying point or conversational centre' of each home.

Chimneypieces could be constructed from a broad range of materials. White, grey or black marble, often with an inlaid relief of exotic coloured marbles, was most sought after – and most expensive. A cheaper and lighter alternative to genuine marble was coloured scagliola, made up of coloured plaster and other aggregates moulded in the form of carved and polished marble. Cast iron fireplaces were very prevalent by 1830, often blacked and decorated with patterned tiles set within the splayed frames.

By 1700 tiles for fireplace surrounds were usually imported from the United Provinces (domestic tile production having largely ceased following the Dissolution of the Monasteries during the 1530s). The characteristic Dutch tin-glazed 'Delft' tile (often termed 'maiolica' after the island of Majorca, a trading centre for tin-glazed pottery) was white, with painted surface decoration in blue or, occasionally, brown. By 1750 a number of English factories were producing large numbers of 'Delftware' imitations; by 1790, however, the new popularity of wallpaper had forced most of these ventures to close. It was only at the very end of the Georgian period that the British tile-making industry was revived. Herbert Minton of Stoke-on-Trent rapidly built up industrial production of medieval-style stamped tiles, with patterns filled with liquid slip and then fired, after 1830. By 1840 the Minton Pottery was producing vast numbers of these indented tiles for fireplace surrounds as well as for floors and walls.

157

Both of these delicate drawing room fireplaces of the mid-18th century have expensive stone insets, on the right, of Italian marble, on the left, of feldspar ('blue john').

A Carron gate of 1825, bought by English Heritage and now in the Red Damask Room at Marble Hill House in Twickenham, Middlesex.

The decorative opportunities of the fireplace tile were not fully exploited until the 1850s; however, another ceramic product was much in evidence on many Late Georgian chimneypieces. By 1800 the Coade factory of Lambeth was marketing a range of 'Coade stone' chimneypieces, made from Eleanor Coade's highly durable ceramic, which ranged in price from an astonishingly cheap 25 shillings each to a by no means ruinous 14 guineas. By far the commonest materials for cheaper fireplaces, however, were plaster and pine. Simple 'Greek' pine fireplaces were offered by Chippendale, Haig and Co. for £1 19s. by the 1780s, while their plaster equivalents could be had for as little as 1s. 6d. each. In 1833 J.C. Loudon reported that plaster chimneypieces were selling in London for 7 shillings, with reeded ones at 28 shillings. Pine examples were invariably painted – usually a broken white (specified by Chippendale himself); they were never left bare, nor subsequently stripped.

THE GRATE

Early in the 17th century andirons or firedogs were first introduced to support burning logs. By 1700 these were also being used to support simple basket grates, and by 1750 the 'stove grate' – a freestanding, rectangular basket with three fire bars placed between two andirons and a grid for falling ash at the bottom – was very common, being found in Chinese, Greek and Rococo styles. Gradually, however, these were eclipsed by the hob grate. This variant first appeared in the 1720s and comprised a basket flanked by flat-topped hobs, designed to keep kettles and pots warm. By 1780 this type had become hugely popular; indeed, original or reproduction examples of these can still be widely found. The hob grate was not, like earlier versions, freestanding, but set into the fireplace, and was available in three basic patterns: 'Bath', 'Pantheon' and 'Forest', each distinguished by the form of the central plate linking the two hobs. A further improvement was the provision of movable iron plates to regulate the size of the chimney opening and thus the efficacy of the updraught – what became known as a 'register grate'.

Even register grates, though, were still smoky and inefficient, with much of the heat disappearing up the chimney flue. By 1810, however, the situation had changed markedly: new, heat-efficient grates were all the rage, and as chimneypieces became simpler in design, the technology of the grate was becoming ever more complex.

The progenitor of the fireplace revolution was the extremely colourful figure of Benjamin Thompson, an American adventurer and amateur engineer who was born in Woburn, Massachusetts but who, having fled to Europe after siding with the loyalist Tories during the Revolution, was awarded the improbable title of Count Rumford by an enraptured Elector of Bavaria in 1784. During a visit to England Rumford was appalled by the primitive condition of the fireplaces he saw, where most of the heat went up the chimney and most of the smoke into the room. The practical result of his concern was the essay 'Chimney Fireplaces' of 1796. This comprised a number of recommendations: a constricted flue throat, to confine the fire to the grate and also to create enough low pressure to promote an upward draught; a smoke shelf to be placed behind the throat, to stop rain and soot falling back down the chimney; a smaller opening for the fireplace as a whole; and angled grate backs and sides, made not of iron (as had been used for hob and register grates) but of a non-conducting material such as firebricks, which would reflect the heat forward into the room.

The effect of Rumford's treatise was instantaneous. New, cast iron 'Rumford' grates were soon being manufactured, while existing fireplaces were modified to fit many of the Count's specifications. Not all his suggestions were immediately taken up, though: the use of firebricks in place of the much-loved iron fireback did not catch on until the mid-19th century.

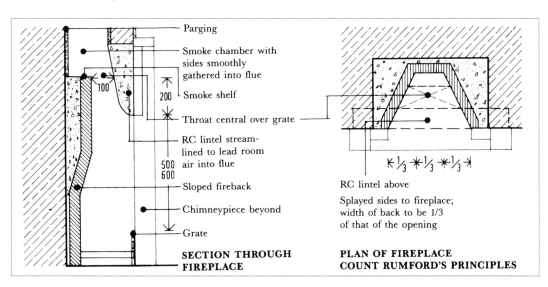

SECTION THROUGH FIREPLACE

- Parging
- Smoke chamber with sides smoothly gathered into flue
- Smoke shelf
- Throat central over grate
- RC lintel streamlined to lead room air into flue
- Sloped fireback
- Chimneypiece beyond
- Grate

PLAN OF FIREPLACE COUNT RUMFORD'S PRINCIPLES

RC lintel above

Splayed sides to fireplace; width of back to be 1/3 of that of the opening

Diagrams showing exactly how a Rumford grate worked, from Edinburgh's The Care and Conservation of Georgian Houses.

FIREPLACE FURNITURE

Late Georgian grates were not intended to be purely utilitarian machines but stylish pieces of room furniture, too. Many of them were provided with applied ornament in brass or steel, while Robert Adam pioneered the use of 'paktong' – an expensive, silvery alloy of copper, zinc and nickel which was not difficult to cast, highly lustrous, easily engraved and did not tarnish. Paktong, brass and steel were, by the 1760s, also used for fenders – a novel fireplace element provided with pierced decoration to match the style of the surround and grate.

By 1830 most of the fireplace furniture we are now familiar with had come into being: coal boxes, shovels, tongs, pokers, fire irons, hearth brooms, decorated bellows and hearth stands. Fire guards, hooked to the top bar of the grate, were widely used, and often decorated with inlaid metal or alloy. Two items common by the 1830s have, though, since disappeared. Fire screens of green-painted silk, rushes or canvas – either self-supporting or, more usually, tied to chair backs – were prevalent, as were bell-pulls, not in themselves connected with the operation of the fire, but invariably placed by the chimney so as to be at the central focus of the room. Bell-pulls, Southey observed, were generally '. . . of coloured worsted, about the thickness of a man's wrist' from which were suspended 'knobs of polished spar' (the 'spar' being, according to Dan Cruickshank, probably of glass).

During the summer, of course, the fireplace could – even in Britain – be dispensed with. The question was then what to put in the gaping hole left by the absence of a cheering blaze. Formerly freestanding grates were simply bodily removed and replaced with a vase of flowers or some such decorative device. With the new, fixed grates, however, a flower vase, or perhaps a decorated folded fan, was lifted inside the grate bars. An alternative solution was to fix a board over the opening; this was often painted with a *trompe-l'oeil* representation of the grate behind – even, on occasion, with illusory flowers – or of the decorative scheme of the room in which it was set, and could be decorated to blend with the fireside dummy boards so popular throughout the Georgian period.

ABOVE: *The art of the chimneyboard is, thankfully, not quite dead.*

RIGHT: *A late Georgian fireplace, from an Islington drawing room.*

THE CHIMNEYPIECE

Repairs to many chimneypieces may require specialist attention. However, some simple tasks can be tackled yourself. Discoloured marble surrounds can be cleaned with a mixture of equal parts of soft soap, quicklime and caustic potash, left several days and then removed. (Lime can now be obtained from a wide variety of sources; do, though, be extremely careful when handling it.) Marble can also be polished with a mixture consisting of two parts soda and water to one part pumice stone and one part chalk. Ingrained dirt on marble or plaster, though, is often best tackled by a professional sculpture conservator.

Blocking off fireplaces can cause serious damp problems within the home, since air can no longer circulate freely and thus moisture is retained. (Remember, too, that most modern houses – with showers, baths, kettles and so on – are far more saturated with moisture than they would have been during the Georgian and Victorian periods.)

THE GRATE

If your iron grate or fireback is rusty, use a wire brush to remove rust and dirt, and clean using white spirit (not water). Steel grates can be cleaned with Solvol Autosol, applied with cotton wool or soft pads.

To blacken iron grates, black lead (Zebrite) is still widely available; alternatively, if you wish to paint the metal, finishes such as Manders Black Ebony paint can be used, applied in a very thin coat. Wax applied to matt black paint can produce an effect resembling black lead; never, though, use a black gloss paint for grates or fireplace furniture.

THE HEARTH

If you have to replace or repair the hearthstone, make sure that the timbers below and the sheet metal which is often inserted underneath the hearthstone are sound, as the principal floor beam often passes directly under the hearth.

SALVAGE AND THEFT

Often you will find that an old house has had its original chimneypieces removed – perhaps only very recently. The choice then is whether to buy a modern reproduction or a salvaged original. Some local authorities are actually now recommending reproductions, given that the recent demand for authentic 'period' features has led to a huge growth in architectural theft.

Many architectural salvage outlets are wholly responsible and impeccably organized; some even compile dossiers on every item they stock. However, the huge increase in the demand for original architectural fittings over the last ten years has led to a proliferation of salvage firms with more dubious pedigrees who do not bother (or want) to check the provenance of the items they receive. As a result architectural theft is big business – and chimneypieces, highly saleable and quickly removed by skilled operators, are at the top of the thieves' shopping list.

There are a number of steps you can take to protect yourself from these increasingly sophisticated thieves:

The sad result of chimneypiece theft: a drawing room in Westminster.

• photograph the fireplaces, and indeed all other interesting architectural features and fittings, and if possible take measurements;

• if the house is being refurbished (the time when the majority of thefts occur), box in your fireplaces, fit alarms if you have not already done so, and let the police know what is happening;

• if there is any building work underway (and particularly if you are away) then ensure that the contractor puts up a prominent sign informing passers-by of the times the site is being worked on, and thus of the times in which any witnessed removal of architectural items is theft.

If you do use a salvaged chimneypiece, establish from the salesman exactly where it has come from. Without precise records of provenance, a salvaged item could well be stolen – and in purchasing it, you are helping to promote the theft of such pieces.

Equally importantly, make sure that the chimneypiece is wholly appropriate for your own home. Oversized and over-elaborate chimneypieces can look ridiculous in a small space. Remember, too, that the position of the fireplace was governed largely by the function, not the appearance, of a room. Thus the less important the room, the smaller and plainer the fireplace. Unfortunately this basic common sense is often forgotten today.

If you do buy a reproduction, ensure that the style as well as the size is applicable to your own home. Many modern 'period' products are sad, clumsy pastiches of genuine historical precedents. Many, too, are in bare pine – in stark contrast to Georgian (and Victorian) practice. Georgian wood or plaster chimneypieces were always painted; stripping historic paint layers away to reveal the basic structure exposes inferior woodwork that was never intended to be seen.

Internal Plasterwork

SOME INTERNAL PLASTERS used a base of lime, like external renders. The final coat, however, frequently comprised a plaster based not on lime but on burnt gypsum (calcium sulphate). Gypsum – originally formed through the action of evaporating seawater – can be found naturally in Dorset, North Yorkshire and in the Trent valley. From the late 16th century onwards it was commonly used to make quick-setting plasters designed primarily for internal use – although it was also used for external decorative effects such as pargeting.

The principal advantage of gypsum plaster – popularly known as Plaster of Paris – was its faster setting time. The raw plaster was mixed with animal hair (usually coarse cow or horse hair or fine goat hair), or possibly with straw or reeds, to make a more durable and more binding substance; the resultant mix was then applied in three or more coats over a network of wooden laths – generally made from deal, fir, beech or inferior oak. In 1727 Batty Langley's *Builder's Chest* observed that there were three types of laths available: 'Heart of Oak', 'Sap-laths' and 'Deal-laths'. Internal plaster was, from the early 19th century onwards, additionally strengthened by the provision of wire netting or by being stapled or tacked to joists – a technique patented in 1797. By the 1850s iron nails were used to provide additional stability for the laths, which now tended to be sawn rather than split; builders also began to make use of the new wire laths.

Gypsum plaster was cast in moulds made of boxwood (or other hardwoods), wax, iron or gelatine. Gelatine had become particularly popular by the mid-19th century as a result of its great flexibility; and both wax and gelatine moulds could, of course, be melted down after use. Today, inevitably, rubber and GRP have largely replaced these traditional mould materials. Rubber 'squeeze' moulds can be used to copy extant designs.

ABOVE: *Delicate plaster ceiling of 1775 – by an unknown hand – from Kenmore in Fredericksburg, Virginia.*

OPPOSITE: *Original pearwood moulds, from The Building of Bath Museum, together with the plaster decorations they produce.*

SCAGLIOLA

Plaster was the principal ingredient in scagliola, a product which when cast and polished looked like marble. Scagliola, made from pigmented plaster and real marble chips, and its cousin Marezzo marble, made purely from plaster, were used not only to save money (being considerably cheaper than the real thing) but also in contexts where true marble, with its great weight, was structurally impractical. Scagliola was used to create anything from 'marble' columns and pilasters to wall panels, chimney-pieces, table-tops and even floors (where, alas, it generally proved far too susceptible to everyday wear and tear).

PAPIER MÂCHÉ

By the end of the 18th century mouldings were increasingly executed not just in fibrous plaster but in lighter and more easily cast derivatives: papier mâché and its superior French relative Carton Pierre (made from pulped paper, glue and whiting). The term 'papier mâché' was first used by the French Huguenot artisans working in east London in the early 18th century. By 1800 the manufacturing base for papier mâché had moved from London's Spitalfields to Wolverhampton, and its quality and durability had improved substantially. Henry Clay's 1772 patent specified a product made from rag paper pasted together, dried on a stove, soaked in oil and then, if a long length was required, wrapped around greased planks of wood. The finished product, painted white or another appropriate colour, or gilded, was much used for complex decoration. In 1827 Nathaniel Whittock noted that papier mâché mouldings and ornaments 'have a beautiful effect on painted ceilings, gilt capitals of columns &c; and the intelligent decorator will see that any clever boy may produce them.'

APPLICATION

Inside the grander houses individual ornaments of gypsum plaster were executed in place by skilled craftsmen. Such work was, however, beyond the financial reach of most households. In the majority of Georgian and Victorian homes pre-moulded ornament, prefabricated in workshops and then fixed on site, was the rule. It was fixed onto the third coat of plaster by means of liquid slip (a thin, dilute plaster), and was on occasion re-pressed when in position to give greater definition. Alternatively, 'press-moulds' could be used to impress patterns upon shapeless masses of wet plaster. Straight cornices and dado rails were usually applied using a specially shaped tool called a 'horse', which could also be adapted to form simple circular mouldings by fixing one end of the tool to the centre of the circle. Pendentive ceiling decorations – particularly prevalent on 'Jacobethan' ceilings of the 19th century – were attached to the main body of the ceiling with wire supports.

ABOVE: *Papier-mâché moulding above the dado. This type of decoration was more common than is generally thought, and is often only discovered during repair.*

BELOW LEFT: *Using a 'horse' to run a plaster cornice moulding. The layers of gypsum plaster are supported by nailed wooden laths.*

FOLLOWING PAGES
LEFT: *Detail of the plaster and wood decoration in Robert Adam's State Bedchamber at Osterley Park. One of the few occasions when decorative plaster reliefs were picked out in another colour was when elements applied onto a coloured ground were highlighted in white, a mid-18th century fashion popularized by Adam and Chambers.*

RIGHT: *This virtuoso plaster ceiling, from the library at Osterley, was designed by Robert Adam in 1766 much in the manner of ancient Roman ceilings. However, few homes could afford decoration of this sort, and most Georgian ceilings remained white.*

169

FINISHES

At least until the 20th century, plasterwork was invariably painted in distemper colours. The disappearance of plaster modelling or wooden panelling above the dado after the mid-18th century resulted in walls which frequently comprised two-thirds plaster and one-third wainscot (wood was still used for the panelled dado and skirting). These two areas were often of subtly different colours, since the pigments used for the distemper paints needed for the plaster were often quite dissimilar to those used for the oil paint applied to the woodwork. Before the advent of chemical dyes in the second half of the 19th century it was simply impossible to use the same pigments for both types of finish.

In more sumptuous Georgian or early Victorian rooms plaster decoration was occasionally picked out in gilt. In general, however, plaster mouldings were painted the same colour as the flat ground – or, in the case of decorative work of Adam's time, painted white. Neither mouldings nor decorative relief work were ever picked out in any colour save white or gilt. Georgian designers relied on the effects of light and shadow to give the mouldings added emphasis, not on the unsubtle application of additional colours to a wall or ceiling that was always designed to be read as one, unified composition.

RESTORING PLASTERWORK

The new owner of an old house may be faced with the task of restoring the character of a building that has lost many of its mouldings – perhaps as a result of conversion, of neglect or of a viciously inappropriate modernization. Where they have been removed, their careful reinstatement can dramatically enhance a plain room.

If no mouldings exist to use as a model for new work, do not despair. If your house is in a uniform terrace or street, it is always worth having a look next door in case your neighbour's home retains any mouldings which have been lost from your own. Beware off-the-peg mouldings, though. While the principle of using prefabricated ornament has been long accepted, few of today's manufacturers can offer a range of plaster profiles which will be wide enough to include designs which are appropriate for the period and scale of your own home. Beyond the most basic skirtings and architraves, many modern plaster products tend to be both historically inaccurate and fairly crude. However, there are some suppliers who can offer a broad range of products and patterns; ask your local district or borough council Conservation Officer for reliable firms.

When replacing plaster mouldings which have wholly disappeared, do not forget that their complexity corresponds directly to the dimensions and the relative social significance of their location. Thus, while drawing rooms on the ground or first floors may feature elaborate cornices and rich, heavy doorcases, rooms at the top of the house may possess only simple box cornices, a rudimentary dado and perhaps no skirting mouldings at all. Decoration is proportional to the pretension of the room; the humbler the function, the more modest the mouldings.

Cracking or bowing plasterwork is a common problem in Georgian homes. All too often the whole wall or ceiling is ripped out, its detailing replaced with off-the-peg plaster mouldings of little character and often of an anachronistic, crude or wholly spurious design. However, with the renewal of interest in restoring old buildings sympathetically there has been a corresponding increase in the number of experts available to help with or at least advise on plaster repair. It is now a simple operation to press a rubber 'squeeze' mould over the remaining ornament to create new work that will harmonize with what is left. Remember, though, that original work, with its subtle patina of age, is always better to look at – and worth more – than a modern replacement; new work will always look new.

If it is necessary to repair or replicate large areas of decorative plasterwork, it is best to consult a recognized expert. If it is an area you can tackle yourself, check before you start that any problems which caused the bulging or crumbling (such as damp or decay) have been properly solved first. The affected area should then be secured by fastening the surface to the supporting timbers with galvanized or nonferrous screws and inserting lime putty behind the plaster. The laths should be examined for rotting, loosening or bad spacing. Then, after cleaning the old plasterwork, a key – preferably of brass screws and woven wire – can be created on the joists prior to application of the plaster. Detailed, step-by-step guides to repair methods can be found in publications such as John Ashurst's 1988 guide for English Heritage (part of the Practical Building Conservation series).

If mouldings are clogged with paint, it is always a good idea to remove this before applying a further covering – but try to keep a small section unstripped, so as to preserve the paint history of the wall or ceiling. The SPAB (see Sources, page 228) produces an excellent advisory leaflet on removing paint from plasterwork. Distempers were traditionally used to paint plaster since they were relatively thin, light and easy to remove. If you can, use distemper today; if not, apply thin coats of non-vinyl or silicate paints. Modern emulsions are apt to obscure plaster detail, and are extremely hard to remove from plaster without destroying the mouldings altogether.

Paint Colour*

WRITTEN DESCRIPTIONS OF 17th-century English interiors are rare, and painters' manuals – aside from John Smith's extremely useful *The Art of Painting* of 1676 – are equally uncommon. However, evidence culled largely from paint sections and laboratory analysis as well as from contemporary paintings suggests that most middle-class interiors of the 17th century were timber-coloured and panelled. The wooden panelling was only left bare (or, rather, covered in a beeswax finish) if it was of fine quality wood. More usually it was painted from cornice to skirting or baseboard in a single, 'wood' colour such as 'oak', 'walnut', 'cedar' or 'mahogany', or, in grander homes, graining. Doors, too, would have been painted this same timber colour. A deeper brown – 'chocolate' or a dark mahogany colour – or even black would have been used for the skirting board; the shutters, too, may have been painted with a darker hue.

White was used for most ceilings from the late 16th century right through to the present century. Remember, though, that Georgian 'white' was not the brilliant, bleached product we know today. Not only was it often 'broken' with a small propor-tion of earth pigments or black to give it a more creamy tone; additionally, the linseed oil which constituted the binding agent for most oil paint – the principal finish used for all internal woodwork – tended to yellow with age. Using a bright, modern white for the exterior or the interior of a Georgian home can look awkward and unsightly.

By the early 18th century colours were used, as Patrick Baty has noted, 'to unify the major architectural elements rather than to subdivide them'. Mouldings were almost never picked out in another colour except in very grand households, where gilt – a far more ostentatious indication of the wealth of the owner – was generally preferred over oil paint or distemper to emphasize the detailing. Walls were decorated according to a strict architectural allegory, the cornice (the equivalent in the hierarchy of the wall to the entablature cornice of the ancient orders) being treated as part of the wall, not of the ceiling.

ABOVE: *A typical (though by no means exhaustive) range of Georgian paint pigments, prepared by Patrick Baty for The Building of Bath Museum. From the top right: white lead, yellow ochre, red ochre, raw umber, burnt umber, burnt Sienna (top middle), Venetian red, red lead, Terre Verte, 'Potter's pink', Naples yellow (top left), smalt, Prussian blue, vermilion and indigo.*

OPPOSITE: *This type of dusty red was considered the best background for prints and for the gilded frames of paintings.*

175

* I am indebted to Patrick Baty for his assistance with this chapter

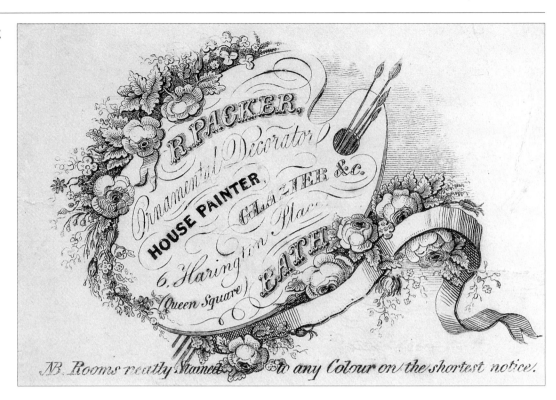

By the 1720s white had become of central importance. Cheap white distempers, made from whiting or chalk and bound with glue, were used for plaster walls and ceilings. But the white colour applied to internal woodwork was an oil paint: white lead. This was far more hard-wearing than distemper – which, being soluble in water, was not washable and tended to brush off with friction. (Up to the 20th century, incidentally, the term 'paint' was applied solely to oil-based colours; 'distemper', based on glue or water, was an entirely different product.) White lead served not only as a colour in its own right but also as the basis for numerous other oil paints. However, making it was a dangerous and messy business. To obtain the highly toxic pigment, large lead sheets would be steeped in vinegar, with the result that 'the corrosive fumes of the vinegar will reduce the superficies of the lead into a white calx which . . . separates by knocking upon it with a hammer,' as John Smith noted. The white pigment was then mixed with linseed oil to make the final paint. To this was often added a small quantity of turpentine in order to give a flat, 'dead' matt finish that would look more like real stone. Flat, matt wall finishes had, incidentally, become prevalent in Britain by the 1740s; in America, though, gloss finishes continued to be applied to internal walls and joinery throughout the 18th century.

By the 1720s Palladian-influenced designers were moving away from the darker, wood colours of the 17th century and towards cleaner, lighter hues. In 1757 Edmund Burke declared in his *Philosophical Enquiry* that 'the colours of beautiful bodies must not be dusky or muddy, but clean and fair. . . . Those which seem most appropriated to beauty are the milder of every sort; light greens; soft blues; weak whites; pink reds; and violets.'

This is not to say, however, that the early Georgians relied on the type of washed-out, pastel shades so often associated in the late 20th-century mind with the interiors of the 18th century. In fact, the Georgians were able to make use of a wide range of both delicate and strong colours. These were usually distinguished in terms of expense, rather than mere hue – an expense which derived from the difficulty, and thus the cost, of obtaining the original pigment from its natural source.

In addition to white, a large choice of cheap, 'common' colours were widely available. These included the whole family of 'stone colours', paints mixed to resemble any type of stone, from a creamy-white 'Portland' to a golden-brown limestone colour. Also remarkably cheap were simple greys such as 'lead colour' and 'French grey', and the traditional brown, timber colours such as oak, walnut, mahogany, 'wainscot' (which was, presumably, usually oak-coloured) and chocolate, still regularly employed for skirtings and internal doors, even if the rest of the wall was in white or stone.

To these 'common' colours could be added other oil colours which were a little more expensive to make, but which were still within the reach of most middle-class households: colours such as 'drab' or 'olive colour', 'pea colour' and 'sky blue'. Still more expensive – at over one shilling per pound – were oil paints such as pink, lemon, orange and 'straw colour'. Such paints could in turn be supplemented by yet more costly oil colours, whose basic pigments were very expensive to extract. These included verdigris, the 'deep fine green' derived from corroding copper; ultramarine, a vivid blue made from crushed and heated lapis lazuli; and smalt, the glittering finish made of powdered blue glass. For those who could not afford ultramarine or smalt, the invention in 1704 of a pigment called 'Prussian blue', named after its country of origin, proved most useful. This powerful pigment, derived from animal blood burnt with alum, was generally available in Britain and America from the 1720s onwards. While cheaper than ultramarine, it was still a relatively costly pigment, and it was only in the second half of the 18th century that strong blues gradually became accessible to the middle classes.

Following paint analysis, the stone colour walls and pale blue mouldings were returned to the large parlour at the Carlyle House in Virginia.

Drab, olive colours, such as seen on the walls in Philip Reinagle's Mrs Congreve with her Children *(1782), appear to have been especially common during the 18th century.*

178

Throughout the Georgian era 'stone colour' was generally held to be most appropriate for the hallway, recalling as it did the grand, stone-built entrance halls of the great houses of the time. Once past the hall, however, stronger colours were frequently preferred. During the third quarter of the 18th century William Chambers was particularly fond of using 'pea green' – a bright green the colour of fresh, not cooked, peas. In 1771 he told a client in London's fashionable West End that 'My intention is to finish the whole in fine stone colour as usual excepting the Eating Parlour which I propose to finish pea green with white mouldings.' By the end of the century green was often favoured for libraries and dining rooms – as were reds, which were generally held to provide the best background for the gilt frames of wall-hung paintings. Reds were, until the invention of chemical dyes in the 19th century, largely obtained from natural plant pigments such as madder, or from brownish earth pigments. Yellows were often obtained from earth ochres, yet could be surprisingly vivid – most notably the highly toxic 'King's yellow' and the 'Patent yellow' used by John Soane at his house in Lincoln's Inn Fields.

The archaeological rediscovery of the ancient world in the second half of the 18th century brought a new and vibrant palette of colours, discovered amid the ruins of Rome and Greece, to the Georgian interior. Lilacs, bright blues and greens, bright pinks and even blacks became highly fashionable. Especially popular was terracotta red ('Pompeian red'), a colour occasionally used in combination with black to create a so-called 'Etruscan' colour scheme based on the decoration of ancient Etruscan pottery. By 1800, too, marbling and graining had come back into fashion, while the heavy gilding which had been such a notable feature of the formal Palladian interior of the first half of the 18th century was largely abandoned. (It is interesting to note that silver was occasionally used in place of gilt decoration by the 1790s. This fashion was short-lived, however, for it was soon discovered that this attractive and lustrous finish tarnished disappointingly quickly.)

By 1770 the application of delicate white decoration, sometimes in relief, onto a wall coloured in rich, Neoclassical tones produced an effect akin to that exploited with considerable commercial success by the potter and industrialist Josiah Wedgwood in his contemporary jasperware. On occasions coloured ceilings, also with white relief, were introduced. Nowhere were ceiling colours more vivid and more daring than in Robert Adam's great houses, where rich lilacs, pinks and greens vied for attention with grisaille panels, plaster cameos or medallions painted with classical scenes by Kaufmann or Zucchi. However, such flights of decorative fancy could only be afforded by the very richest patrons. In practice, most ceilings of the later 18th century remained white – although the Regency period did witness a brief fad for blue-and-white 'clouded' ceilings.

Sash windows were often painted white, both outside and in. However, by the end of the 18th century green, grained, brown and even black sashes appear to have been common, especially when those windows were sited in the context of a pale-coloured external stucco. Other internal woodwork was also finished in a colour from this range, while internal and particularly external ironwork was on occasion painted blue – smalt or Prussian blue, if this could be afforded, or indigo if it could not. (As early as 1703 Neve's *City and Country Purchaser* was recommending the blue-grey oil paint obtained by blending indigo with white lead as the best cheap covering for domestic

Terracotta-and-black painted designs, featuring suitably antique motifs, on the walls of Adam's celebrated Etruscan Room at Osterley Park.

ironwork.) Alternatively, by the end of the 18th century ironwork could be painted with a 'bronze green', designed to imitate ancient, patinated bronze, or possibly with a dark, 'invisible' green. Darker greens were used to help external railings, gates, fences or iron garden furniture blend in with the verdant background; John Pincot's 'invisible green' of 1811, for example, was explicitly designed to be 'agreeable when relieved by verdure and vegetation'. The use of black paint for ironwork, however, is a comparatively recent innovation, dating from the late 19th or perhaps the early 20th century. Front doors – invariably set in a stone-coloured architrave – seem to have been of any dark colour, of which brown, black, dark red and green were generally the most common.

RE-CREATING INTERNAL PAINTWORK

There are no easy set formulae for Georgian colour schemes or combinations, nor standardized recipes for particular colours. The British Standard system is a very recent one; what Georgian commentators described as 'stone colour' or 'wainscot colour' could vary enormously in hue. Thus, within certain parameters, Georgian room colours remain largely a matter of personal taste. Internal paints, for example, may simply have been chosen to match the colour of the furniture and fabrics in the room.

Houses regularly open to the public represent a helpful source of re-created historic paints. However, remember that the scale of, and the money originally expended on, the treatment of a room in a grand building may be quite inappropriate for a more modest Georgian home. Your own decorative schemes should not necessarily imitate those of great houses such as Kedleston or Mount Vernon.

Remember, too, that each material used in decorating or furnishing the interior possessed its own range of colours. While there was some overlap between these, they could not always be transposed from one medium to another. To make use of the Georgian ceramic colouring popularly known as 'Wedgwood blue' in painting a wall, for instance, is not a safe way of attempting to re-create typically mid-Georgian wall colours. Even the pigments that were used in traditional distemper – the soft matt finish, made largely from pigmented whiting and glue, which was generally used for painting plasterwork – could not necessarily be used in oil paints. As Patrick Baty has remarked, blue pigments such as blue verditer 'were generally reserved for use in distemper, being liable to darken and go green in oil . . . whose linseed oil content, particularly in areas deprived of light, caused it to yellow with age.'

When attempting to discover original paint colours, bear in mind that what you apparently see from a cursory examination may be very misleading. Since linseed oil

ABOVE: *Marbling pilasters, part of a scheme to re-create the interior of the York Cemetery Chapel of 1837.*

LEFT: *Some typical items that you might see on an 18th-century grinding slab, as prepared by Patrick Baty. From the left, anticlockwise: azurite (a blue mineral pigment used in distemper); 'dragon's blood resin', obtained from the root of an Asian tree, which is then dissolved in turpentine, alcohol or linseed oil and used for varnish; a stone muller, with crushed cochineal beetles – used to make an extremely expensive red; 'mountain green', ground from malachite; and rose madder, an expensive pigment obtained from the root of the Asian madder plant.*

OPPOSITE: *Chocolate-brown seems to have been by far the commonest colour for internal doors and skirtings during the 18th century – a sharp contrast to the late 20th century's belief that all old woodwork should be painted bright white.*

183

yellows when in the dark, what you may think is, say, a green may actually have been a blue. At the same time, direct light can have varying effects on different media. For example, at Boston's Harrison Gray Otis House conservators found that window- and lamp-light had bleached the oil in the original oil paints faster than they had the Prussian blue pigment, making the yellowish-green paints which contained an element of Prussian blue far lighter and much more blue.

The real nature of the original paint can thus only be determined via the microscopic examination of a paint section, taken by an experienced paint restorer, which incorporates all the historic paint layers from a given point. Amateur paint scrapes may reveal a colour that has actually been changed with age, or with exposure to the chemicals contained in the succeeding paint layer, and will fail to register properly the effect that treatments such as transparent glazes – liable to have been lost, or to be read as a separate application – may have had on the original paint finish. Sometimes the undercoat may be mistakenly interpreted to have been the final finish. So, if you do want to determine exactly what colours your wall has been painted, it is best to consult a recognized expert, and to submit a paint section to the laboratory.

RESTORING INTERNAL PAINTWORK

Traditionally, glue-bound soft distempers (not to be confused with the more modern, water-bound 'hard distempers') were used to paint internal plasterwork. There were sound practical reasons for this: they were cheap, quick to apply and, being loosely bound, they could be easily washed off for renewal. This was especially useful in the context of plaster mouldings, which could easily become obscured by repeated coats of paint.

Today, however, distemper has largely been replaced by modern emulsions, layers of which will rapidly clog up moulded plaster detail and will be extremely difficult to remove. (The best way of removing emulsion from plaster is to use gentle steam pressure and a palette knife; this, though, remains a very painstaking process.) It is therefore preferable to use distemper, rather than emulsion, for repainting plasterwork, as it can be easily removed using warm water and a soft brush.

Stripping is always advisable in order to clear away old paint layers which obscure detail. However, in eradicating accumulated areas of paint you are also removing all traces of paint history – making it impossible for future owners to discover the exact character of historic colour schemes. For this reason try, when stripping, to retain a small unstripped area. Never use a blowlamp or a blowtorch: countless fires in Georgian homes both large and small have been caused in this way. Instead use hot air or steam strippers, or non-alkaline solvents.

Once stripped, the wood or plaster surface should in nearly every case be repainted again. Despite many modern myths, Georgian woodwork was almost never left bare; only very expensive woods such as seasoned oak or imported mahogany would have been left visible – and even then they would have been protected by layers of beeswax. The widely held – and wholly mistaken – belief that stripped pine is historically appropriate for old buildings appears to derive from a confusion of genuine historic practice with the 20th century's obsession with 'honest' materials, and in particular from the post-war enthusiasm for Scandinavian stripped pine (or indeed the more recent enthusiasm for unpainted tropical hardwoods).

In re-creating old colours, it is often very difficult to recapture the true nature of the Georgian paint finish. Dragging and stippling do very little to mimic the 'ropey' nature of Georgian paint; instead, they always look very much what they are – modern decorative techniques. At the same time, few householders will now be able to use lead-based oil paints for health reasons. If the status of your building does allow you to use lead paint, then even the method in which your pigment is ground may produce a distinctly modern effect. As Patrick Baty has remarked: 'Pigments ground by hand affected the appearance of oil paint, their non-uniform particle size both producing an unevenness of colour and also influencing the way light was reflected, causing the surface to look more lively than a modern, highly refined product.' Even the brushes have changed: the flat brushes we generally use today are a late 19th-century innovation. It is therefore perhaps best to rely on a modern reinterpretation of Georgian paint application, rather than to attempt to return to the 18th century.

RESTORING EXTERNAL PAINTWORK

It is always advisable to leave brickwork unpainted. Modern oil-based paints and emulsions are generally impervious to water; if they crack (which they will do as the masonry moves and settles), water can penetrate into the bricks behind but will be unable to evaporate out through the paint. The result will be that even newly applied paint will quickly fall off – making painted brickwork a very high-maintenance covering – while the brickwork behind will be eroded through the action of rainwater and its soluble salts.

One coloured finish for bricks that will allow the wall to breathe properly is pigmented limewash. This traditional covering can still be made; a guide on its preparation is produced by the SPAB (see Sources, page 228).

Painted stucco walls, as we have seen, need repainting about every three to five years, to stop water from entering the fabric through cracks in the paint film. Whatever colour you decide to repaint with – remembering that original stucco colours were often far darker than today's ubiquitous pale creams – never use a brilliant white, which is not only historically inappropriate but can create a hideously glaring effect. Some local authorities, such as Hove or Westminster, actually recommend specific BS-numbered cream colours for stucco, so consult your local Conservation Officer if in doubt as to what would be best.

Lastly, however you decide to repaint your house, remember that in Britain Listed Building Consent is legally required 'for the painting or repainting of the exterior or interior of a listed building which would affect the character of a listed building'. So think again if you are contemplating painting your Georgian house pink and black.

---- ◆20◆ ----

Wallpaper

MUCH HAS BEEN DONE over the last ten years to remedy the lack of information about historic wallpapers. The Victoria and Albert Museum and the Whitworth Gallery in Britain, and America's splendid Winterthur Museum in Delaware, all have fine collections of old papers. However, despite the leading part Britain played in the development of the wallpaper industry in the 18th century, the only museums in the world actually devoted to wallpaper are to be found not in Britain (or America) but in France and Germany. Thankfully, though, Britain is beginning to follow the US's lead in boasting a growing number of firms specializing in traditional wallpaper manufacture and in historic wallpaper conservation.

Wallpaper appears to have originated in China around the 3rd century AD. The earliest Western wallpapers yet found, however, date from only the 16th century; the oldest wallpaper in Britain (at Christ's College, Cambridge), whose pattern imitates Italian damasks of the period, is dated at *c.*1509.

Wallpaper was a more sophisticated form of wall decoration than the hand-painted or stencilled patterns that had been applied directly onto plaster for centuries. This is not to say, however, that the application of wallpaper entirely replaced these techniques. Stencilling in distemper colours – a practice which has recently undergone an enthusiastic revival – was, for example, commonly used on the floors and the walls of American homes throughout the Georgian period, although in Britain the practice of stencilling remained largely limited to rural cottages. In both countries wallpapers, too, were still being hand-coloured by 1780. Indeed as the duties imposed on printed wallpapers accumulated, hand-colouring – which avoided any such taxation – became increasingly attractive, especially for poorer households.

Most of the early English papers were simple black-on-white designs. As paper was scarce and therefore expensive, these black patterns were often printed not onto virgin white paper but onto the reverse sides of book proof sheets, onto leaves from

OPPOSITE: *A modern reinterpretation, by de Gournay, of an 18th-century Chinese wallpaper design.*

187

condemned titles, or even onto older wallpaper sheets. (The latter were generally used for lining boxes or drawers rather than hung on the wall.) If the printed papers were to be coloured, they were colour-washed by hand.

Early patterns – often imitations of more expensive wall coverings such as silk damask or embossed leather – were either hand-painted, stencilled or block-printed onto the paper with wooden blocks (usually made of elm). Flower designs were particularly common in England, as were simple geometric shapes, such as diamonds or stripes, and cartouches.

In block printing, the initial drawn pattern was committed to rough paper, which was then cut into small squares to facilitate blockmaking. The colour was applied to the blocks, which were then either hammered into place on the paper or set between two rollers fixed in a frame. The paper itself was generally made from shredded rags, broken up through the action of water and rollers (often by being passed through an early 18th-century machine known as a 'Holland beater'); paper pulp was not widely used until the early 19th century. The resultant mess was then moulded into thick paper.

Block-printing wallpaper in the traditional fashion.

Early 18th-century woodblock-printed patterns were heavy and pasty, and executed in distemper colours thickened with glue (size). In 1691 William Bayley had received government assistance for his invention of brass blocks, but little was subsequently heard of his innovation, and metal pressing was not properly introduced until the 19th century. Yet despite Bayley's failure Britain led the way in wallpaper technology throughout the 18th century. John Baptist Jackson (1701–77) was the first to use oil-based colours rather than distemper, in order to produce more intense colours and greater accuracy in patterning. In 1754 Jackson published the first book in English to deal with wallpaper: *An Essay on the Invention of Engraving and Printing in Chiaro Oscuro.* Although this was a thinly disguised advertisement for the products of his own wallpaper factory at Battersea, Jackson's designs were particularly well drawn, and had a substantial influence on later papers. His pioneering use of oil colours, however, was less successful; he asserted that they would 'never fly off' and that 'no water or Damp can have the least Effect', but unfortunately these claims proved far too optimistic, and oil colours never truly caught on.

Wallpaper was, from the end of the 17th century, sold in lengths made up of sections about one yard long, glued end to end. By 1712 the length of the complete roll (or 'piece') had become standardized at twelve yards.

Technological advances, though, gathered pace as the century wore on. In 1753 Edward Dighton devised a rolling mill to print engraved black and white papers; these copperplate papers were, however, still hand-coloured. In 1764 Thomas Fryer, Thomas Greenhough and John Newberry patented the first cylinder-printing machine, which could print coloured fabrics as well as coloured wallpapers. And in 1774 production of papers was improved still further by the introduction by A.G. Eckhardt of a device, based on woodblocks, to transfer designs made on squared paper quickly and easily to the wallpaper. It was not until the 19th century, however, that printing with metal plates – in use since the 1760s – was widely practised. Manufacturers were quick to take up Edward Cooper's 1816 patent for producing a continuous length of paper. Yet it was only the appearance in 1839 of Harold Potter's power-driven rollers – printing four colours, and able to remove surplus ink as they printed – that the age of mass-produced wallpaper could be said well and truly to have begun.

This stunning pillar-and-arch paper, shown in Philip Hussey's interior of the 1750s, may be a little overpowering for modern tastes, but certainly testifies to the use of highly architectural wallpaper designs by the middle of the 18th century.

By 1760 papers were printed with a wide variety of patterns. Particularly popular were the architectural papers which featured repeated Neoclassical motifs such as urns, swags and niches, sometimes enhanced by built-up layers of papier mâché to suggest wood or plasterwork. Printed architectural forms were also used to create newly popular print rooms, where engraved views, arranged symmetrically on a strongly coloured ground, almost covered the wall above the dado. Perennially popular, though, were simple, repeating patterns using one or two colours and, perhaps, additional stripes; by 1830 they were extremely common in both British and American households.

Although simple, repeating patterns are still highly popular today, the same cannot be said of every Georgian wallpaper design. One enthusiasm that has certainly not survived into the late 20th century is the mid-18th century passion for flock wallpaper. Today flock has distinctly downmarket overtones; in the Georgian era, however, it was all the rage on both sides of the Atlantic, and was hung in the most important rooms of the house. The flocking technique of sticking powdered wool to glued paper in order to present the effect of cut-pile fabrics must have been widely practised by 1626, for in that year Charles I issued the Paper Stainers Company with a monopoly on the production of flock papers; yet the oldest surviving flocked wallpaper in Britain, found at the Ivy House in Worcester, dates only from *c.*1680. By the 1730s William Kent was using flock papers to replace the grand textile hangings in the Great Drawing Room at Kensington Palace, a royal home much used by George II, and British flock paper was being exported not only to the colonies but also to France, where 'Papier d'Angleterre', as it was known, was soon the height of fashion.

A refinement of the flocking process produced 'lustre paper', made by sprinkling powder paints or powdered glass, rather than wool offcuts, onto a glue pattern. Whereas only the most expensive flocks were printed in more than one colour (Thomas

Bromwich of Ludgate Hill in London is known to have printed a number of double-colour flocks for Chippendale), lustre papers could be printed using a variety of colours and textures, and even combined with flocking.

For those who could afford it, highly expensive, hand-painted Chinese papers represented the acme of taste. Imported in large quantities from China during the 18th century by the East India Company, they were often confusingly termed 'India Papers', after their importer. Chinese designs were non-repeating, and generally featured some combination of birds, fishes, flowers or landscape – often arranged to tell a simple story. For those who could not afford genuine Chinese papers, however, there was an alternative: English 'chinoiserie' papers, with their heavy outlines, repeating motifs and cramped arrangement of subjects. Few of these survive today, and thus they are, ironically, often more highly prized than the Chinese models they sought to imitate.

Protective trade barriers ensured that few European papers entered Britain and (at least before 1783) the colonies. In 1773 the official ban on foreign 'painted' papers – originally imposed during the 1480s and still in force, although the government had long exempted the East India Company's Chinese trade – was finally repealed. However, a customs duty of 11s. 2d. (raised to 13s. 4d. in 1777, to help pay for the American war) was immediately applied to all foreign papers – again, excepting those imported by the East India Company. There was also a levy exacted on native papers. A

Modern designs such as this – Zoffany's 'Bokhara' – attempt to mimic those Georgian damask papers and flock papers which in turn sought to suggest damasked fabrics.

191

wallpaper tax had existed since 1712, when it stood at one penny per square yard; by 1809 it had been raised to one shilling, and was only finally repealed in 1836. As with all matters to do with the defence of private property, wallpaper taxation was taken very seriously; as late as 1806 the forging of a wallpaper tax stamp was made a capital crime.

The taxation of imported papers – as with that of so many other luxury goods, which had to be imported from Britain or in British hulls – hit the American colonies especially hard. America had to rely solely on imported English and Chinese papers until 1765, when John Rugar established a wallpaper factory in New York. Predictably, though, the Revolution provided a much-needed boost to native manufacture: by 1790 there were wallpaper factories established all along the eastern seaboard. It had also become possible to import French products.

DISCOVERING WALLPAPER

Old wallpaper can be found in a surprising number of locations, such as behind skirting boards, architraves and built-in cupboards, as well as in more obvious places such as behind plasterwork or panelling. If you do find old paper, but do not want to keep or match it, remember that a future owner of the house may wish to do so. It is thus most helpful if you can preserve the paper in some form, or can photograph it if it has to be removed.

Reproduction wallpapers at Temple Newsam House, Leeds, produced by Zoffany from originals found at the house.

*Zoffany's 'oak garland'
paper, found at Temple
Newsam as a gold-and-
pink design (dated at
c.1790), but here
reproduced in yellow and
white.*

REMOVING WALLPAPERS

Some of the earliest wallpapers were directly tacked onto plaster. By the mid-17th century, though, they were more often set on a wooden frame stretched with canvas. This helps the restorer enormously, since the cavity between wall and canvas has kept the paper dry and reasonably intact.

By the early 18th century papers were glued onto the canvas, which was in turn tacked or pasted onto the plaster wall. (Printed borders were often used to hide the tacks or the glued edges.) The canvas backing allowed for easier removal and rehanging – a vital factor given the expense and fashionability of some papers – and also helps the modern restorer. By 1800, however, canvas linings had fallen out of fashion. Both this development and the Regency fad for varnishing papers (a process which can seriously affect colour tones) do not make the modern wallpaper restorer's job any easier.

If you find that the old paper is glued directly onto plaster, it can be eased off with a flat-bladed knife. If it is attached to wood, however, it is best to remove the whole element, wood and all, since any attempt at separation can cause irreparable damage. Wallpaper can be steamed off, but this is a complicated procedure which can easily end in disaster; it is therefore safer to consult a recognized conservation expert before beginning.

If you would like the sample you have salvaged to be reproduced for the rest of the wall, try to ensure that a fairly large piece – preferably about twenty square inches – is rescued. Samples destined for reproduction should ideally be taken from a point near the cornice, dado rail or skirting so that any bordering that survives will be included. Once they have been removed from the wall, keep samples out of bright light. Ensure,

193

Modern interpretations, by Zoffany, of (left) a French 18th-century design by the great master of wallpaper manufacture, Jean-Baptiste Reveillon, and (right) of an early 19th-century Chinese paper.

194

too, that they are kept flat: if rolled in the manner of modern papers, the delicate fragments may crack and break. If you are left with a number of wallpaper layers stuck together, these can be steamed apart (again, a task best done by a recognized expert) or manually separated after a brief soaking in lukewarm water, which dissolves the glue before the paper colours. But make sure that these layers are kept in sequence, so as not to confuse any dating.

DATING WALLPAPER

If you cannot date a paper from the pattern, there are other methods you can use. The colour itself may provide a clue. Blue papers, for example, might well date from the first half of the 18th century, when there was an ineffective embargo imposed on the use of any colour but blue in fabrics and papers – a measure designed to protect the native indigo dying trade and to prevent the import of French fabrics (both of which it signally failed to do).

It may also help to look at the structure of the paper itself. Thin, friable, brownish paper with slightly dragged patterning probably dates from the 19th century and is machine-printed. Thicker paper with watermarks, horizontal joints, tax marks (see below) and thick printing with a lip suggests a hand-blocked, 18th-century paper. Remember that in the Georgian era most wallpapers were sold as joined sheets, pasted together before printing and sold in a 'piece' or roll, usually about twelve yards long.

Imperfections in the colours may also help determine the printing method, and thus the date. Tiny air bubbles, introduced during block-printing, are often discernible in the thicker colours on old papers; the thin colours of the 19th century, on the other hand, are often streaked. European colours tended to run when paste was applied underneath the paper, and it was only in the 1780s that the French began to introduce Chinese-type insoluble dyes. Unfortunately, the pioneer of this technique, Jean-Baptiste Reveillon, had his factory razed by the mob during the tumults of 1789.

If you are lucky enough to find a tax or date stamp on the reverse side of the paper, this will date it rather more precisely. After 1714 the penny duty on wallpaper, first imposed in 1712 to help pay for Marlborough's celebrated but costly victories in the War of the Spanish Succession, was recorded by the monogram 'GR', together with code letters whose significance is now, alas, unknown. Other tax stamps may also help. In 1716, for example, a First Account stamp was introduced, while in 1773 a duty stamp appeared on all foreign papers except those imported by the East India Company. From 1778 each sheet of imported wallpaper was stamped twice, once at either end, and from 1786 a 'Duty Charged Remnant' stamp was added. Some foreign imports even carry a stamp indicating the port at which the paper entered Britain.

MATCHING WALLPAPERS

In the past ten years a number of firms have appeared which are able to restore and match historic wallpapers from existing fragments. Details of these can be found from national or local museums dealing in old wallpapers, or from specialist bodies such as The Wallpaper History Society (set up in 1988 and based at London's Victoria and Albert Museum).

When seeking to reproduce old papers, do not forget that the colours you see may have faded considerably since the paper's installation – most historic paper colours tend to oxidize to green or brown if left constantly exposed. The original tones may still be detected under paper borders commonly used above the dados and other continuous mouldings. Once again, though, always contact an expert first; time spent doing this will save a lot of money and heartache later on.

21

Curtains, Shutters and Blinds

TIMBER COVERS FOR window openings have been in use for centuries. Before the introduction of affordable glass – windows only began to be widely glazed in the 16th century – they provided the only real defence against the elements. Timber mullions and transoms were covered in wood, waxed paper, oilcloth or skins, which were in turn often protected with a primitive wooden shutter of the ledged-and-battened variety. The introduction of glass into domestic fenestration made external shutters no less essential. Early Georgian crown or cylinder glass could only be manufactured to form relatively small panes, and was still comparatively fragile. Wooden shutters were still needed both outside and inside the house, to protect the glazing, to keep out draughts, to eliminate light, to deter intruders, and to retain heat.

By 1700 sash windows were invariably fitted with interior shutters. (External window shutters and storm windows are discussed above, in chapter 10.) In the most important rooms these fittings were panelled to match the adjacent mouldings, and installed in recessed shutter boxes which were either placed at right angles to the window or, increasingly, installed in a splayed fashion in order to maximize the amount of light entering the room when the shutters were open.

Internal shutters of the Georgian era were often divided into two or even three separately hinged sections. This arrangement allowed some daylight to be admitted to the room (via the open, upper sections) while at the same time ensuring that valuable fixtures and artefacts were still protected from the harmful effects of direct light. Alternatively, removable shutters or screens covering only the lower portion of the window area could be fitted into position after the fixed shutters had been completely opened. These small shutters or 'snob screens' were invariably painted green. When they were used in combination with fixed shutters, curtains and sub-curtains, the resulting melange succeeded in preventing the prying eyes of the curious or envious from glimpsing the interiors of the fashionable.

OPPOSITE: *Half-closed shutters at Elder Street, Spitalfields. Partly closing shutters not only helped to keep out the curious gaze of passers-by, but also to protect valuable furniture and fittings from the harmful effects of direct light.*

199

By the early 18th century, internal shutters were often operated by small brass rings. Today many of these have disappeared, forcing the user to manhandle the shutters themselves. However, other items of shutter furniture often do survive, particularly the staunch, wrought iron bars which both held the closed shutters in place and helped to defend the windows from forced entry, and the more delicate brass or iron hooks.

Security was of course always a prime consideration for the Georgian houseowner. In the 18th and 19th centuries many shutters were actually equipped with bells – a primitive but highly effective ancestor of the modern burglar alarm. Other householders relied wholly on the horizontal stay bars, or yet more sturdy pullbars (removable iron bars which were slotted into holes either side of the shutters), to deter thieves.

It is always worth retaining any original closing mechanisms that remain attached to old shutters. Not only do flimsy, modern brass catches look inappropriate on heavy Georgian or Victorian shutters; putting original or reproduction iron bars back also helps create a good security barrier. You may even want to put back shutter bells – a step which has recently been taken at the splendid Soane Museum in London's Lincoln's Inn Fields.

By the early 19th century a number of ingenious solutions had been found to the problem of where to stow internal shutters when space was at a premium. In many homes, for example, shutters were not stored in shutter-boxes at each side of the window, but disappeared vertically into specially constructed cavities in the sills below – being retrieved by means of the brass handles fixed to the top of each shutter.

BLINDS

Window blinds were employed not to retain heat – shutters could do this far more effectively – but to prevent direct light from fading precious furniture, fabrics and paintings during the daytime.

Regency designs for painted window blinds from Edward Orme's Transparent Blinds *(1807).*

*Half-drawn Venetian
blinds, from a Regency
watercolour.*

The first patent for a painted cloth blind was granted in 1692, to William Bayley. Primitive roller blinds comprised little more than a strip of cloth nailed to a wooden cylinder; by 1700, however, more sophisticated spring-loaded canvas or cloth blinds, often known as 'spring curtains', were already widely available. The material, attached to the tin case which housed the spring, was often dyed or painted green. By 1808, however, George Smith was recommending that roller blinds be painted 'of the same colour as the principal draperies'. Even such an august craftsman as Thomas Chippendale was not beneath supplying houses with roller blinds: in 1776 his men spent ten days repairing the blinds in just one house. However, despite their widespread use during the Georgian period, few original roller blinds survive today.

The same can be said of Georgian Venetian blinds. Made from painted deal laths held by cloth tapes, these had reached Britain and America by 1760. Their name may not have originated from any Venetian provenance, but from their early use to mask Venetian windows – a characteristic, three-light opening very popular with the Palladian designers of the first half of the 18th century. Annabel Westman notes that

201

in 1762 Vile and Cobb invoiced Lord Coventry 'For one Italian Blind with a Circular Head to Do for the Venetian Window in your Study, with Silk lines, and Tapes, and a Man's Time fixing'. An advertisement of *c.*1766 bravely extolled the virtues of the Venetian blind, declaring that it 'draws up as a Curtain, obstructs the troublesome Rays of the Sun in hot weather, and greatly preserves the Furniture, prevents being overlooked, & may be taken down or put up in a Minute.' Yet its reliability was often disappointing: roller blinds were notoriously fragile, but these early Venetian blinds proved equally faulty, the laths easily becoming dislodged from the tape that held them.

External roller blinds, drawn up into painted wooden blind boxes, were popular by 1800. The boxes themselves often survive today, but it is extremely rare to find an extant exterior blind. From the evidence we do have, it seems that they were made of very heavy-duty canvas, and were often decorated with gaily coloured stripes.

SUB-CURTAINS

Behind the curtain itself many Late Georgian households installed a muslin 'sub-curtain'. Its primary function was to keep direct light out of the room during the daytime, and thus to help protect valuable furniture, fabrics and paintings from fading.

Originally only imported into Britain and the colonies from India (the East India Company being able to import them without incurring the usual taxation), muslins were woven in Britain after 1779, following the invention of the spinning mule. They were made from very finely spun cotton, and could be of a variety of consistencies, from cambric to dimity. Today, however, the term 'muslin' is reserved for what the Georgians would recognize as a plain, gauze-like white cambric.

CURTAINS

Only grand Early Georgian homes possessed fine window curtains. More modest households made do with white or undyed stuffs tacked or hung inside the window – or more often than not dispensed with such pretentious trappings altogether. These simple cloth hangings were often tied back during the day, and the tacking at the top of the window frame hidden behind a valance.

By the 1730s, however, window curtains were of prime significance in the domestic interior. They could be drawn horizontally, along a rod, or vertically, using cords, and could be in one or two pieces. Of the vertically drawn forms, the 'festoon' was, by 1760, evidently the most popular both in Britain and America. In 1765 Benjamin Franklin declared that 'The Fashion is to make one Curtain only for each window', indicating that the festoon had eclipsed both the two-part pull-up version and draw curtains in popularity. Although festoons probably originated in France, and were accordingly termed 'French curtains' by some, across the Channel they were, confusingly, known as *rideaux à l'italienne*. Since festoons were devised to be drawn up vertically in swags, they were made of light fabrics which could be raised with little effort. The lines which pulled the curtains ran through two vertical lines of brass rings on the back of the material, over boxwood pulleys hidden behind a pelmet or board, and down – via lead plumbets to help them hang properly – to be fastened near the dado rail.

Festoon curtains drawn at the Gardner-Pingree House in Salem, Massachusetts.

An alternative to the festoon was its near relation, two-part drapery curtains. These operated on roughly the same principle as the festoon: the two pieces of material were drawn up vertically towards the outer corners of the window, resulting in heavy swags at both sides. To neaten the effect, raised drapery curtains were often fastened at dado level by large metal cloak pins, which served to prevent the material dangling down towards the floor in an unsightly fashion, while the ends of the operating cords generally culminated in decorative tassels. Textile historian and curtain authority Annabel Westman has found few references to this type of curtain before the 1750s; yet in 1758, she notes, Vile and Cobb were fitting up Croome Court in Worcestershire with a 'Green Lutestring festoone curtain, Slitt up the middle, Lin'd & fring'd Complete', and by 1767 leading cabinet-makers Thomas Chippendale and John Linnell were both referring to this type of two-part form as 'drapery window curtains'.

Even in the Georgian era, however, fashions came and went with alarming frequency. By 1780 enthusiasm for both the festoon and the drapery curtain was fading fast. The latest vogue was now for 'French draw' or 'French rod' window draperies. In this arrangement a pair of curtains drew not vertically but horizontally, the two pieces of material being attached to a rod above the window architrave (which could itself be hidden by a pelmet) by wooden or brass rings. 'These curtains are still in use in bed-

203

Designs for window displays from Sheraton's Cabinet-Maker and Upholsterer's Drawing Book *(1791–4).*

rooms', remarked Sheraton of festoons in 1803; but he noted 'the general introduction of the French rod curtain in most genteel homes'. French rods represent the immediate ancestor of today's horizontally drawing curtain display.

For those who wanted a more ostentatious arrangement than French rods could provide, Regency Britain boasted a far more elaborate style of decorating windows: the drapery display. By 1810 some large rooms were being fitted with what was called 'continuous drapery', where vast swathes of fabric ran in massive swags from pelmet to pelmet. In extreme cases even the ceiling was draped, creating the effect neatly described by the contemporary term 'tent-room'.

CURTAIN FABRICS

As the Georgian period progressed, curtain materials became increasingly lightweight, to allow for easy operation. 'Tabby' curtains were especially popular during the first half of the period; tabby was a striped silk, with alternate satin and watered stripes, which was often dyed gold. Alternatively, traditional moreens could be used. These fabrics were lined either with a simple, light cotton or with tammy, a light but strong worsted material which, like chintz, could be glazed to make it yet more resilient and lustrous.

By the last quarter of the 18th century the whole family of furnishing fabrics was being revolutionized as a direct result of Britain's rapid industrial advance. In 1770 Hargreaves' spinning jenny, allowing eight spindles to be wound at the same time, was patented; nine years later Samuel Crompton's 'mule' (named after the principal power source of the early 18th century) combined Hargreaves' invention with

Arkwright's rollers in one machine. And after 1781 James Watt's steam engines began to be harnessed to both the mule and the spinning jenny, facilitating faster and less labour-intensive production.

This industrial progress effected lasting changes in the home. New, lighter cottons and linens could now be manufactured faster, and more cheaply, than ever before. Printed patterns were now within the reach of everybody – not just the privileged few. Even previously expensive fabrics such as silks were no longer the preserve of the rich. In every type of house traditional fabrics such as velvet – a notoriously heavy dust-collector – were replaced by materials that were both lighter in weight and easily washable – the latter being an important consideration in the dirty, newly industrialized cities of Britain and America.

The greatest revolution came in the use of cotton cloths. Since 1722 no one had been permitted to wear printed or dyed calico cottons, or to use them for covering furniture, since their importation from India threatened to undermine the native British industry, which in turn relied increasingly heavily on exports to the American colonies. In 1774, however, this restriction was removed for British cotton calicoes, although the ban on Indian imports persisted. In order to tell British from Indian cloth, the former was now made with three blue lines running through the warp – a device which makes detection and dating far easier for today's textile scholars.

The immediate result of the 1774 Act was that British cottons were in widespread use by 1785 as curtains, bed-hangings, seat upholstery and loose covers. Chintzes were especially popular. Their colourful, large scale, flowered patterns, often derived from Chinese silks, could withstand repeated washings without fading. Home-made calicoes, too, with their small scale patterns, were equally bright and resilient.

By 1778 block-printed cottons were very prevalent on both sides of the Atlantic. In many houses they were substituted for traditional silk or worsted damasks as upholstery for seat furniture. In 1759 George Washington showed he was very much in tune with contemporary furnishing fashions by ordering from London 'a Tester Bedstead', from whose cornice was hung 'Chintz Blew Plate Cotton furniture' designed to match the wallpaper sample he had sent with the order.

At the time Washington made this order, and for the next twenty years, America remained entirely reliant on Britain for sophisticated textiles, as it was for nearly every element which went to furnish the fashionable house. This dependency only began to be broken after the conclusion of the War of Independence in 1783; even then, the American writer Tench Coxe noted in 1794, 'we manufactured less at that time than any other nation in the world', and necessarily remained 'the first customer for British manufactures'. Some attempts were, however, made to establish a native textile industry before the end of the war. Clearly the most determined of these pioneers was the textile printer John Hewson, who, as Florence Montgomery relates, packed up his Philadelphia factory in 1777 in the face of the advancing British, was captured, and, escaping from custody in 1779, set up a new calico printing works – despite the fact that 'the savage foe of Britain' had 'made such a destruction of their works and materials'.

Before the 1750s textiles were printed in the same manner as wallpapers, with pearwood or sycamore blocks. Dots at the corners of each block pattern served as registration marks for placing the next block by hand. By 1770, however, copper plates were widely used. They were far larger than wood blocks – generally about a yard square –

and, although at first unable to print more than one colour, were by the later 1780s printing two- or three-colour designs. The principal colours chosen were usually red (obtained from the dye produced by the madder plant), black, blue, purple or very occasionally yellow. In 1765 Richard Baucher of New York advertised 'red, blue and purple copperplate furniture, calicoes and chintz', recently imported from London. The patterns printed in these colours were naturalistic scenes, often landscapes, much in the vein of hand-painted Chinese wallpapers. And following the introduction of printing by copper rollers by Thomas Bell in 1783, the way was open to yet more sophisticated, multi-colour printing.

By 1785 linens, cottons, silks and other furnishing fabrics were increasingly coordinated with the rest of the room – a novel doctrine which took some time to gain wide acceptance. In 1758 Benjamin Franklin, then resident in London, told his wife that he had bought '56 yards of cotton printed curiously from copper plate, a new invention, to make bed and window curtains' and also seven yards of the same pattern for 'chair bottoms'. 'These were my fancy', he explained, 'but Mrs Stevenson tells me I did wrong not to buy both of the same colour.' A year later George Washington's copper-plate bed-hangings were, in contrast, expressly designed to match the colour and pattern of the wallpaper, the festoon curtains and the bed coverlet, in order to make the bedroom 'uniformly handsome and genteel'. By 1765 Franklin had learned his lesson and was ordering, through his son, 'three curtains of Yellow Silk and Worsted Damask' to match chairs already covered in yellow damask.

SHUTTER REPAIR

If your house has its original shutters, it is important that they be kept in working order, and used as often as possible. Window shutters are the most effective way of prolonging the life of a room's furnishings.

Wooden shutters are often susceptible to dry rot. To prevent this, ensure that the mouldings and flashings on the outside of the window are doing their job properly, and that water is not being admitted into the wooden members of the sash. Regular operation of the shutters – and regular opening of the windows themselves – also helps to encourage a free flow of air, which can go some way towards preventing decay.

If your shutters are infected by dry rot, ask an experienced local joiner to replace the affected area with pre-treated timber. Surrounding members should also be provided with anti-fungal plugs. Remember, though, that once the source of the water penetration has been dealt with, there should be no recurrence of the problem; similarly, if the basic problem is ignored, no amount of chemical treatment or wood substitution will help eradicate the infection in the long term.

Window shutters were never left unpainted during the Georgian or Victorian periods. The fashion for exposing internal woodwork derives more from late 19th-century Arts and Crafts theories and from the post-war fashion for stripped Scandinavian pine and 'honest' materials than from genuine Georgian practice. The idea of stripping the paintwork from old pine shutters in order to reveal the inferior, knotty grain of the wood below would undoubtedly horrify Georgian designers.

If you are painting or repainting the shutters, a useful rule of thumb is to choose the same colour as the window surround – which in most cases will be white. Remember,

OPPOSITE: *The re-created draperies in the Green Pavilion at Frogmore, Berkshire. The form of the curtains has been taken from the depiction of the room included in Pyne's* Royal Residences *of 1819, while the chintz pattern is a design of 1804. Green velvet has been used for the borders, and green tammy for the lining.*

too, that the bright, bleached whites which are so commonly used for historic properties today are very much a 20th-century innovation. Georgian designers and decorators
always used creamier, off-white matt oil paints, which tended to yellow with age, for
most of the internal woodwork. The harsh glare of modern bright white paints is inappropriate for such old surfaces.

It is also worth retaining any original closing mechanisms that remain. Not only do
flimsy modern brass catches look inappropriate on heavy Georgian shutters; putting
original or reproduction iron bars back also helps create a good security barrier.

CURTAIN REPAIR

Protection   Textiles are easily damaged by direct light. The fabric both fades and rots –
and neither of these processes is reversible. So, if you have valuable old curtains, it
makes sense to treat them as reverentially as possible.

While few houseowners will want to install the type of complex lighting controls
now common in large historic houses open to the public – where a limit of 50 lux or
less is often imposed – this does not mean that nothing can be done to stop undue
decay. Ensuring that furniture is not pressed up against the curtains helps to guard
against unnecessary wear and tear, as does limiting over-frequent handling. In addition, try not to have old curtains gathered in tie-backs too often, since this fashion
causes undue stress on the fabric. Leaving curtains to hang free and unfettered when
you can is always a good idea for delicate old textiles.

Installing a plain sun-blind or sun-curtain – the modern equivalents of the muslin
sub-curtain – behind the main drapes helps to protect the lining from excessive fading. This type of protection can be seen in many houses in the care of the National
Trust and English Heritage.

Cleaning   Do not be tempted to clean valuable old curtains yourself, or to entrust
them to dry cleaners, no matter how many claims they may make as to their reliability
and experience. Only recognized textile conservation experts have the skill to clean
old curtains without damaging them. (A list of the leading textile conservation centres
can be found on page 231.)

Simple dust removal can be effected once every one or two years with a gentle,
domestic vacuum cleaner, adjusted to its least powerful level. (The National Trust recommends the Hoover Dustette.) Once again, though, take care not to handle or dis-
turb the fabric too much. And be careful of tassels or fringes, which may be prised
loose by the cleaner's suction.

Repair   If you have Georgian curtains which need repairing, never attempt to do this
yourself, no matter how expert you may be. Countless historic textiles have been permanently damaged by well-intentioned but harmful and irreversible home repairs. As
with cleaning, it is always best to entrust the repair of historic textiles to a recognized
conservation expert.

Storing   If you are storing or moving old curtains, there are a few key guidelines to
bear in mind. Firstly, never fold the curtains, or they may hole or tear; always roll them
up, using tissue paper to separate the surfaces. Ensure, too, that the paper is non-
acidic, otherwise the acid may in time help to decay the material. The same applies to
the cardboard box in which you store your curtains: this, too, should be acid-free. And

ensure that no metal pins are included in the package as they can rust and damage the fabric, nor any rope or string, which can bite into the fragile surfaces. The store-room itself should be dark, free of pests and of a relatively constant humidity.

RE-CREATING HISTORIC CURTAINS

Curtain-making can be extremely rewarding, especially if it is helping to re-animate a sense of your home's historic past. However, if you are planning to create 'period' curtains for a Georgian interior, it is wise to abandon a few popular myths.

The most commonly held of these is that the festoon curtain (or 'ruched blind' or 'Austrian blind', to give it just two of the many names used today) is appropriate for windows of all periods and sizes. The basic principle of the festoon curtain was to let the maximum amount of light into the room by gathering the curtain material into the awkward space between the window architrave and below the room's cornice. Unfortunately, this simple idea is one that is often lost on professional and amateur decorators today. Festoons are made not only of heavy, bulky materials, but are allowed to obscure most of the window even when they are raised. The result is often that the whole of the top sash frame is unseen behind the folds of frilled fabric.

Other general misconceptions regarding size, pattern and colour also need to be dismissed. In the same way that chimneypieces and mouldings varied in size and design according to the wealth of the household and the function and relative size of the room, so Georgian curtain displays were always designed to correspond with the purpose and dimensions of the room in which they were hung. The more modest the room, the plainer and more reticent the curtains would have been. A lavish, elaborate and over-sized festoon arranged in the middle of what would have been a small bedroom makes no decorative sense at all, as well as looking quite ludicrous.

In addition, remember that – as with so many aspects of the Georgian house – the belief that there was one particular 'Georgian' style or approach to curtain design is quite wrong. There are countless 'Georgian' patterns, dating from c.1710 to c.1830, which varied enormously according to the location, size and social pretention of the house (a fashion that was being introduced in a London pattern-book one year may not have reached the provinces until ten years later).

A large number of books exist which can guide you through the intricacies of curtain-making. As long as you bear in mind the particular requirements and history of your own room, re-introducing period curtain designs should prove an immensely enjoyable experience. Many of the curtain materials made more widely accessible as a result of the Industrial Revolution can still be easily bought today; chintzes and linens, for example, can be obtained at any department or decorating store. Accessories such as Georgian-style curtain rods, cloak pins and tassels are also widely available. Unlike other aspects of the Georgian house, Georgian window treatments can be re-created with comparative ease, and at little expense.

Floor Coverings

FITTED CARPETS ARE by no means a 20th-century invention. By the mid-18th century the new fashion for fitted carpets – carpet strips cut to accommodate the shape of the floor – had made fancy floor parquetry or surface decoration quite redundant. In 1756 Isaac Ware noted that 'the use of carpeting at this time has set aside the ornamenting of floors in a great measure; it is the custom almost universally to cover a room entirely; so that there is no necessity of any beauty or workmanship underneath.' Fifty years later Sheraton observed that 'since the introduction of carpets, fitted all over the floor of a room, the nicety of flooring anciently practised in the best houses, is now laid aside.'

Oriental luxury carpets first appeared in Britain, it is believed, during the Crusades. By 1600 Turkish imports were being augmented by carpets from Persia; at the same time, the first attempts were being made to copy Middle Eastern carpets here in Britain. Yet throughout the 17th century carpets remained rare items, gracing only the homes of the very rich. Given their expense, they were more usually used to cover tables than floors. With the expansion of Britain's trading empire after 1713, however, this situation improved markedly: luxury carpets were now more widely available in Britain, and becoming increasingly less expensive. In 1749 the architect John Wood remarked that, during the past two decades, 'as the new Building advanced, Carpets were introduced to cover the floors.'

During the latter half of the 18th century the technological impetus of the Industrial Revolution provided a further boost for the British carpet manufacturers and a great increase in carpet ownership. By 1820 even the notoriously extravagant George IV was buying mostly British carpets for his new Royal Pavilion at Brighton. And by 1840 British knotted or pile carpets, made by machines able to copy the intricate geometric patterning of the traditional oriental products, were to be found in countless households. No longer were the great country houses the only places to find luxury textile floor coverings.

ABOVE: *A Brussels carpet, dating from 1757, from the Exeter factory.*

OPPOSITE: *The knotted carpet in the Red Drawing Room at Syon House, Middlesex, designed by Robert Adam and made by Thomas Moore at the Moorfields factory in 1768–9.*

211

The first truly commercial carpet workshop appeared in Britain in 1735, in Kidderminster, Worcestershire, where both pile and flat carpets were made. Five years later a workshop was set up in Wilton, Wiltshire, at the instigation of the 'Architect Earl', the 9th Earl of Pembroke; this was designed to manufacture pile carpets alone. By the mid-1750s factories making Turkish-style knotted carpets were established at Moorfields in London, at Exeter and, in 1755, at Axminster in Dorset. Axminster knotted carpets were soon known for the quality of their design, which relied on both Turkish and Persian influences as well as fashionable Neoclassical motifs. In 1787 Abigail Adams – soon to be America's First Lady – visited the Axminster factory and declared that 'The carpets are equally durable with the Turkey, but surpass them in colors and figure.'

Axminsters were substantially cheaper than their Levantine models; nevertheless, they were still beyond the reach of most households. Far more affordable were the woven carpets of Wilton and Kidderminster. These were made on looms, the worsted warp being brought to the surface to form a looped pile (a so-called 'Brussels' carpet), which was often subsequently cut to give a velvet-like texture (creating a 'Wilton' carpet). Brussels and Wiltons were not only cheaper than knotted carpets; they were also more versatile. Initially woven in strips up to three feet wide, they were usually provided with frequently recurring patterns which allowed them to be cut to cover all manner of room dimensions.

UTILITARIAN FLOOR COVERINGS

Harder wearing than the pile carpets was the family of reversible 'ingrain' carpets. These were popularly known as 'Kidderminster' or 'Scotch' carpets; a factory opened in Kilmarnock in 1760, and by 1800 their manufacture was based at a number of Lowland towns. Made by intersecting two webs of cloth, using the same basic principle as that used in the weaving of damask cloth, the back would have exactly the same pattern as the front, only with the colours reversed. In 1822 the Kilmarnock factory began experimenting with three-ply ingrains. These were more complex and colourful, with backs and fronts that were wholly different.

Ingrain carpets (not made since the beginning of the 20th century) were popularly regarded as coarse and cheap; yet they served very well as utilitarian coverings for hallways, servants' rooms and stairs. One variant of the ingrain was the so-called 'Venetian carpet', woven in Britain and the US (but never, it seems, in Venice) from c.1800. These flat-woven carpets had weft threads which were so tightly packed that they actually obscured the warp. They can often be recognized by their customary simple, striped pattern.

Even more basic and more common than ingrains were druggets, and the whole family of related floor and carpet covers. Usually in green or brown, druggets could be made of baize (a heavy woollen cloth), serge (a twilled worsted fabric), haircloth (spun animal hair combined with a linen, cotton or wool warp), or similar heavy-duty materials. Their principal function was to protect fine luxury carpets from dirt or wear, and they were often attached to floor studs to prevent them becoming wrinkled. Druggets were also used to catch crumbs, falling soot or hair powder. In poorer households, of course, they were used as substitutes – not as covers – for good carpets.

Ingrain carpet in the Little Parlour at Mount Vernon, Virginia.

213

Re-created Georgian floorcloths at the John Marshall House, Richmond (above), and the Carlyle House, Alexandria (below). Geometric patterns were particularly popular for floorcloth designs.

The alternative to the drugget was the simple painted floorcloth or oilcloth. Very popular throughout the 18th and 19th centuries, very few floorcloths, alas, survive today. They were made by wetting canvas or a similar cloth, applying a number of coats of paint, and then perhaps stamping a pattern on with wood blocks. They were often painted to imitate expensive flooring materials such as black and white marble, inlaid stone, 'tessellated pavement' (a fragment of which still survives at Calke Abbey in Derbyshire) or oak boards. They could even be painted to resemble oriental carpets: in 1771 a Boston painter was commissioned to paint four yards of floorcloth in 'Turkey Fatchion'. The designs could also be figurative: von Rosensteil and Winkler cite the example of a Boston order of 1788 for 'a Poosey-Cat on one Cloath and a leetel Spannil on the other'. Or they could be simply of one, flat colour; Thomas Jefferson, for example, commissioned 'a canvas floor cloth, painted green' for the South Dining Room at Monticello. As Dr Ian Bristow has noted, floorcloths did not generally last very long, and by 1800 many tradesmen also offered a profitable sideline in 'Old Cloths new Painted and Repair'd'.

There were other utilitarian alternatives to the floorcloth. In his 1833 *Encyclopaedia* J.C. Loudon mentions the 'paper carpet'. No examples survive of this, but it was probably a cheap floorcloth made by sewing together pieces of paper with rough cloth, and oiling, painting and varnishing the result. Like oilcloths, paper carpets could be rolled up and stored. A more robust alternative was the 'list carpet': a home-made covering made up of fragments of cloth (which formed the weft of the weave). List carpets were particularly common in American homes, where they were also known as 'selvedge' carpets, after the fabric borders which so often featured among the components.

Additionally, the strong interest in chinoiserie in the years before 1800 brought with it a sudden revival in the provision of oriental-style floor matting. Reed, cane or rush matting was no longer used only in the humblest cottages and farmhouses; in 1759 George Washington ordered 'Canton' matting for his Virginia home of Mount Vernon, while thirty years later the Prince of Wales was introducing rush matting into the sumptuous Great Drawing Room at Carlton House. Matting was generally woven in strips three feet wide, which were then stitched together to form larger carpets.

It is useful to remember that nearly every item of importance in the middle- or upper-class Georgian interior was, from the mid-18th century onwards, provided with a protective cover. As we have seen, druggets were often used to save expensive carpets from daily wear and tear; at the same time, servants were well briefed to keep direct light away from valuable floor coverings and furniture by closing the shutters or the muslin sub-curtains. In 1851 Elizabeth Gaskell even noted the practice of 'cutting out and stitching together pieces of newspaper so as to form little paths to every chair set for the expected visitors, lest their shoes might dirty or defile the purity of the carpet'.

Rush matting in Martha Washington's bedroom at Mount Vernon.

A Persian carpet of the 18th century, of the type imported by well-to-do British and colonial families for both floors and tables. This example is now in the Cecil Edwards Collection at the Victoria and Albert Museum.

The removal of carpet and furniture covers was a good indication of how exalted the visitor was.

Clearly such protective measures are not very practicable today. However, if you have an expensive carpet, it is sensible at least to try to keep it away from sources of direct light for much of the day. If your old carpet is in need of repair, it is best to approach a recognized conservation expert.

If laying or relaying a carpet, remember that the back needs as much protection as the front. The carpet weave permits dirt to filter through to the floor below; once at floor level, however, the dirt can wear away the back of the carpet, ultimately causing a disintegration of the fabric. To prevent this happening it is vital to ensure that the carpet has some sort of padded backing. Only floorcloths were traditionally laid without backing.

───── 23 ─────

Lighting

MOST GEORGIAN INTERIORS were dark and gloomy. After sunset the only illumination available to most people before the end of the 18th century was either a dim, unreliable oil lamp or erratic, guttering candles. As Dan Cruickshank noted in *Life in the Georgian City*, 'prodigality with candles was not the Georgian rule and the average room was very underlit by the standards of the 19th and 20th centuries.' A recent study by the University of Pennsylvania (quoted in Roger Moss's *Lighting for Historic Buildings*) found that, in the period 1775–1800, Philadelphia homes possessed on average eight candles in the house, while homes in rural Bucks County had on average only one or two which were usually kept in the parlour or kitchen. When Mrs Delany visited Holkham Hall in 1774 she was aghast to find that even 'my Lady Leicester works at a tent-stitch frame every night by one candle that she sets upon it, and no spectacles.'

The source of this candlelight was usually the wall – either in the form of candelabra on side tables or wall-mounted sconces. Sconces were often fixed in front of mirrors, so as to reflect more light about the room; the circular, convex mirrors so popular after the 1760s provided a particularly effective way of distributing light in this manner.

The simplest form of candle was the rush light: a dried rush dipped in animal fat, held in a simple clip mounted on a stand. On the New England coast they also used 'candle-wood', cutting the locally abundant, resinous pitch-pine into rough candle shapes, which were then anchored in the fire-grate or placed in a crude iron or tin holder. As early as 1642 one of the first colonial settlers admitted of candle-wood that 'I cannot commend it for singular good, because it droppeth a pitchy kind of substance where it stands.'

More expensive than rushlights or candle-wood were tallow candles, made from rendered animal fat. James Mease's American edition of A.F.M. Willick's *Domestic Encyclopaedia*, published in Philadelphia in 1804, details their laborious manufacture,

OPPOSITE: *A rushlight, mounted in a simple, early 18th-century iron holder.*

219

noting that 'Good tallow candles ought to be made with equal parts of sheep and ox-tallow; care being taken to avoid any mixture of hog's lard, which occasions a thick black smoke, attended with a disagreeable smell, and also causes the candles to run.' Unsurprisingly, tallow not only burnt badly and smelt strongly, but was also difficult and messy to make into candles. Having been partly purified by being melted onto and skimmed off boiling water, tallow was subject to further processing: 'To purify the tallow still more', declared Mease and Willick, 'it is strained through a coarse horse-hair sieve into a tub; where after remaining three hours, it becomes fit for use.' The tallow was then either moulded into a candle shape, or a wick was dipped into the hot fat.

An alternative to tallow, available in New England and other areas where whaling had become the dominant industry, was spermaceti – the fatty substance found in the head of the sperm whale. Spermaceti candles, although still smoky, were often considered superior to tallow ones. They were made in similar ways, either by dipping the wick in the melted spermaceti, or by moulding candles in multiple moulds made of tin or brass. By 1730 the streets of Boston were lit by series of tin lanterns containing a single spermaceti candle, while in 1748 an advert in the *Boston News Letter* lauded the spermaceti candle for serving 'the use and purpose of three tallow ones' and for producing a 'Dimension of the flame nearly four times more'. Not all householders greeted them with enthusiasm, however. In 1804 Mease and Willick warned readers that 'spermaceti candles are subject to the greatest waste of any [candles] and emit more smoke than tallow candles, although their vapor causes no disagreeable smoke like them.'

Wax candle and candlestick at the John Marshall House, Richmond, Virginia.

Yet more expensive (costing on average three times more than tallow) and more effective were beeswax candles. (In 1710 beeswax candles were taxed at 4d. a pound, tallow at only ½d. a pound.) Beeswax which smelt less, smoked less and had a higher melting point than tallow or spermaceti could only be afforded by the rich. And even in grander houses it was possible to determine a guest's relative importance by whether wax, spermaceti or tallow candles were being provided. (Temple Newsam's invaluable catalogue *Country House Lighting* cites an example from the 1770s, when the butler at Leinster House publicly embarrassed the new tutor by asking his mistress whether he was 'to have wax candles or tallow'.)

Good quality beeswax was not a native product either in Britain or in America, so had to be imported; thus candlemaking firms were generally situated in ports. In America the wax was often of a greenish colour, and on both sides of the Atlantic wax was frequently dyed red, yellow and black as well as green.

The Georgian candlestick epitomized, perhaps more than any other single item, the taste and craftsmanship of the period. By the mid-18th century silver, pewter, glass or porcelain candlesticks were widely available. Of these, the silver candlestick or candelabrum – a strong, distinctly architectural composition, with clean lines and minimal detail – became one of the most popular domestic status symbols. After *c.*1760 it most commonly took the form of a fluted stick, perhaps with a Corinthian or palm-leaf capital, and a pyramidal or domed foot. The silversmiths of Sheffield came to specialize in candlestick production, industrial innovations of the 1760s such as die-stamping allowing the constituent parts of the candlestick to be assembled far more simply and cheaply than before. By the turn of the century, however, the ceramic candlestick had become the most popular form of candleholder. Porcelain was not only cheaper than

Girandoles and candlestands from Thomas Chippendale's Gentlemen and Cabinet Maker's Directory *(1754).*

silver and metal alloys, but also easier to maintain, while advances in ceramic technology meant that increasingly finely detailed examples could now be made for a very reasonable price.

For those who could afford them, elaborate chandeliers were widely available by 1730, made of glass, wood or metal (brass examples had been in occasional use at least since the 15th century). Of these materials, glass, being the best reflectant, was also the most popular; made in Britain from *c.*1720, by the end of the 18th century glass 'lustres', as they were often called, had become vast and elaborate compositions. During the 1780s the Prince of Wales bought over £4000-worth of massive glass chandeliers, made by the renowned manufacturer William Parker, for use at Carlton House. When not in use, these grandiose, gravity-defying confections were wrapped in fabric to protect them from summer flies.

Candles, whether in the context of elaborate chandeliers, sinuous girandoles or simple candlesticks, remained a very important part of the domestic interior throughout the whole of the Georgian period. By 1837 oil and gas lamps still remained relatively expensive, and candles were often used to augment lamplight or gaslight. Candles were only truly banished from the domestic interior with the advent of electric lighting at the beginning of the 20th century.

221

OPPOSITE: *Two-branched girandole of c. 1775 from 7 Great George Street, Bristol.*

Light fittings from Temple Newsam House, Leeds. RIGHT: *a brass chandelier of 1738;* BOTTOM RIGHT: *Wedgwood candlesticks of the 1780s;* BELOW: *mahogany lampstand of c.1830.*

OIL LAMPS

For most of the 18th century oil lamps were dirty, smoky and unreliable, being dependent on oils that were both messy and inefficient. Before the 1780s, indeed, oil lamps were rarely used in Britain, although in the New England ports whale-oil lamps (which made use of an important by-product of the local whaling industry) were common by 1750. Many of these lamps were not only inefficient but also highly dangerous – particularly those lamps which used a mixture of 'camphene' (turpentine) and alcohol, a fuel that was notoriously prone to spontaneous combustion.

By 1840, however, the methods of lighting both house interiors and town and village streets had undergone a dramatic revolution. These technological developments, moreover, profoundly influenced the way in which interiors were disposed and decorated and the manner in which indoor and outdoor activities were planned.

The first major breakthrough was the invention of the Argand lamp. In 1783 the Swiss chemist François-Pierre Aimé Argand (1750–1803) patented a new form of lamp, generally known in Britain as a colza-oil lamp after the thick, greenish-yellow rapeseed oil it burned. (Argand lamps in the United States continued to use traditional whale oil until the mid-19th century, rape being an uncommon crop on the western side of the Atlantic. Arthur Hayward has noted that between 1800 and 1845 over 500 patents were granted for Argand-style whale-oil lamps in the US.)

Argand's lamp was constructed around a revolutionary new circular cotton wick with an internal air channel and a larger surface area from which to burn the oil. The wick itself was placed in a funnel (originally of iron, later of glass) to help promote the upward flow of air. A further distinctive element was the oil reservoir, installed halfway up the side of the funnel so the thick oil could flow down to the bottom of the wick.

An Argand lamp, as shown in The Penny Encyclopedia *(1839).*

A design by J.B. Papworth (1803) for a three-tiered brass chandelier incorporating oil lamps.

Although initially rejected in France, the invention was enthusiastically taken up across the Channel. Matthew Boulton agreed to manufacture Argand's lamps, and following the lapse of Argand's temporary patent in 1786 imitations began to flood onto the market. An 1800 inventory of Washington's home at Mount Vernon, Virginia, included a number of Argand lamps, and by 1820 Argand lamps were fairly common in the wealthier homes and were appearing in the pages of influential publications such as Rudolf Ackermann's *Repository of the Arts*. As Elspeth Moncrieff has noted: 'Suddenly a light was available which produced ten to twelve times the light of a single candle, transforming the activities which could be carried out after darkness.'

225

A colza-oil lamp of 1838, from Temple Newsam.

Argand lamps were made from a variety of materials: an observer of 1786 noted 'crystal, lacquer and metal ones, silver and brass and every possible shade'. They could be many-branched; some metamorphosed into full-blown (if rather ungraceful) chandeliers. In 1809 the 'sinumbra' or 'astral' lamp solved the problem of the bulky, shadow-casting reservoir, the oil being passed through tubes in the rim of the lampshade, which in turn enabled the reservoir to be removed. (One of the initial promoters of this development was the indefatigable American inventor-adventurer Benjamin Thompson, Count Rumford – see page 161.) Yet there was still the problem presented by the physical nature of the thick, sluggish colza oil itself. During the 1820s a Frenchman, Franchot, invented an ingenious spring-loaded piston to pump the oil into the wick; his lamps were soon known as 'moderateurs', after the name of the valve needed to control the oil flow. By this time, too, the safety match had appeared (1824), allowing for easier lighting of these increasingly sophisticated lamps. It was not until the 1860s, however, that a more refined, less viscous substitute was found for colza or whale oil: paraffin.

GAS LIGHTING

Shortly after the Argand lamp first appeared, a new technological wonder helped to brighten the streets and homes of Georgian Britain. In 1787 Lord Dundonald became the first individual to install coal-gas lighting in his home. Twelve years later William Murdoch of London established the first factory to produce coal-gas, while in 1799 the Frenchman Philippe Lebon registered the first patent for a gaslight. The most important breakthrough, though, came in 1803, when Frederick Winsor erected the first public gas lights in Westminster's Pall Mall and also fitted up his own house with one-and-a-half inch gas pipes. Winsor – an extrovert refugee from Moravia – subsequently shot to prominence through a well-timed marketing stunt: illuminating the facade of Carlton House with gaslight for the King's birthday. Encouraged by an admiring Prince Regent, in 1812 Winsor founded the Gas-Light and Coke Company at Cannon Row in Westminster; from there he pumped gas to light such prominent landmarks as Westminster Bridge and the Drury Lane Theatre. Two years later additional gasworks were opened in Shoreditch, Spitalfields and Finsbury, and by the mid-1820s Winsor was supplying gas to 70,000 domestic and street lamps in the capital. The first gas street lighting in America appeared in 1817, in Baltimore.

The pace of progress did not instantly solve every lighting problem. The brightness of the gas lamps could not be increased; thus there simply had to be more of them. More seriously, the new gas piping inside the home was often carelessly buried under only a thin layer of plaster, or sited adjacent to heat sources or main passageways. As a result, gas explosions were by no means uncommon during the 1820s and 1830s. Nevertheless, gas lights remained a vast improvement on both candlelight and oil lamps.

DAYLIGHT

The Georgians were very sensitive to the detrimental effect of direct light on their important furnishings, and went to great lengths to minimize its effect during the day. By the later 18th century muslin sub-curtains – often with an embroidered border – helped filter the harmful light entering via the window. Shutters or blinds, too, were often pulled during the day so as to preserve the furniture and fabrics. Even relatively modest, middle-class households retained servants who could be employed to turn furniture out of the sun, to apply furniture covers when necessary, and to safeguard carpets with druggets or 'paper carpets'. The absence of such hired help in the 20th century has, inevitably, allowed many Georgian fittings to deteriorate rapidly in recent years.

MODERN LIGHT FITTINGS IN OLD HOMES

Today, original gaslights or oil lamps are very hard to find, and are usually prohibitively expensive. The introduction of electricity at the end of the 19th century caused most original Georgian light fittings to be heavily adapted, wholly replaced, or crudely ripped out.

This view of the famous Chippendale desk in the library at Temple Newsam shows how dramatic the effect of bleaching by direct light can be. Compare the faded woodwork of the top drawers with the original wood colour of the hidden drawers below.

In lighting a Georgian interior (or indeed any historic room), simplicity and sympathy are the key prerequisites to bear in mind. Often it is better to buy simple, modern fixtures, which do not seek to deny their contemporary design, rather than to install elaborate 'period' reproductions of doubtful historical worth. In general, the type of pseudo-historical and over-bright brass light fittings which so frequently dominate modern 'period' re-creations are to be avoided.

Most Georgian lighting was wall-mounted. Again, however, this historic effect may be impossible to recapture; even reproduction sconces and girandoles often prove very expensive. A good compromise between the practical needs of a modern household and the aesthetic requirements of an old interior is to provide freestanding lamps, which do not dominate the wall surfaces and which can be removed or replaced at will.

It is also a good idea to install light switches immediately above the dado, rather than at head height, as it makes these fixtures less obtrusive, and easier to operate. It may be preferable, too, to buy switch surrounds made not of bright brass, nor of white plastic, but of a more visually sympathetic medium such as wood or perspex; these can now be found in a variety of outlets.

While bogus 'Georgian' or 'Victorian' light fittings abound, good modern reproductions of genuinely historic models – from simple brass chandeliers to Neoclassical pewter candlesticks – are now becoming more widely available, and at an affordable price. As with so many aspects of equipping the Georgian interior, the best advice is simply to shop around – and not to be taken in by over-enthusiastic claims of historic pedigree. You may find that you have more success rummaging in junk shops and salvage outlets than in visiting period lighting showrooms.

Sources of Information

UNITED KINGDOM

Local Authorities

The Conservation Officer of your local district or borough council (usually part of the council's Planning Department) is there specifically to help houseowners on all aspects of period house renovation. He or she may be able to recommend good, reliable craftsmen in your area, and can also let you know about possible local authority grant aid for repairs or alterations. If your building is listed, he or she should also be able to provide details of the listing, which should tell you more about the history of your home. Some county councils also have expert conservation staff.

English Heritage

English Heritage (429 Oxford Street, London W1R 2HD, tel. 0171 973 3000) is the principal body regulating the conservation and maintenance of historic buildings in England. English Heritage (officially known as the Historic Buildings and Monuments Commission) also has equivalents in Wales (Cadw) and Scotland (Historic Scotland). All three bodies are able to advise on grant aid and on Listed Building Consents.

National Amenity Societies

The National Amenity Societies not only serve as legal consultees on alterations to listed buildings, but also offer advisory services on all aspects of period homes, whether listed or not.

The Georgian Group (6 Fitzroy Square, London W1P 6DX) deals with the period *c.* 1700 – *c.* 1837. The Group provides advisory guides on key aspects of the Georgian house and general booklists for those beginning or contemplating repair or redecoration, and gives advice on matters of refurbishment and redecoration.

The Society for the Protection of Ancient Buildings (37 Spital Square, London E1 6DY, tel. 0171 377 1644) specializes in the medieval and early modern periods up to *c.* 1700. The Society also publishes a series of invaluable technical pamphlets and more basic information sheets on most aspects of maintenance and repair, and can advise on suitable surveyors and craftsmen.

The Victorian Society (1 Priory Gardens, London W4 1TT, tel. 0181 994 1019) advises on the period 1837–1915.

The Council for British Archaeology (Bowes Morrell House, 111 Walmgate, York YO1 2UA, tel. 01904 671417) deals with archaeological finds and industrial archaeology of all periods.

The Ancient Monuments Society (St Ann's Vestry, 2 Church Entry, London EC4V 5HB, tel. 0171 236 3934) deals with buildings of all periods, particularly churches.

Suppliers

The author and publisher do not expressly recommend the suppliers listed below, nor intend this list as an exhaustive guide, but include the following addresses for general information.

Brickwork

The Brick Development Association, Woodside House, Winkfield, Berks SL4 2DX, tel. 01344 885651.

The Construction History Society, c/o The Chartered Institute of Building, Englemere, Kings Ride, Ascot, Berks SL5 8BJ, tel. 01344 23355.

Traditional Brick and Tilemakers

Aldershaw Tiles, Kent Street, Sedlescombe, Battle, East Sussex TN33 0SD, tel. 01424 754192.

Blockleys, Sommerfeld Road, Trench Lock, Telford, Shropshire TF1 4RY, tel. 01952 251933.

Bovingdon Brickworks, Pudds Cross, Ley Hill Road, Bovingdon, Hemel Hempstead, Herts HP3 0NW, tel. 01442 833176.

The Building Centre, 26 Store Street, London WC1E 7BT, tel. 0171 637 3166.

W.H. Collier Ltd, Marks Tey, Church Lane, Colchester, Essex CO6 1LN, tel. 01206 210301.

Freshfield Lane Brickworks Ltd, Freshfield, Dane Hill, Haywards Heath, Sussex RH17 7HH, tel. 01825 790350.

Ibstock Building Products Ltd, Ibstock, Leics LE67 6HS, tel. 01530 260531.

Keymer Brick and Tile, Nye Road, Burgess Hill, Sussex RH15 0LZ, tel. 01444 232931.

Michelmersh Brick and Tile Company Ltd, Hillview Road, Michelmersh, Romsey, Hants, tel. 01794 368506.

Northcot Brick Ltd, Blockley, Moreton-in-Marsh, Glos GL56 9LH, tel. 01386 700551.

Tarmac Bricks Ltd, Chancel Lane, Pinhoe, Exeter, Devon EX4 8JT, tel. 01392 466561.

The Tiles and Architectural Ceramics Society, c/o H317, H Block, Centre for Cultural and Education Studies, Leeds Metropolitan University, Calverley Street, Leeds LS1 3HE.

Stonework

English Heritage Building Conservation Training Centre, Room 528, 429 Oxford Street, London W1R 2HD,
tel. 0171 973 3821.

The Lime Centre, Long Barn, Morestead, Winchester, Hants SO21 1LZ, tel. 01962 713636. Courses on repointing, flint walling and making and examining lime mortar.

The Stone Federation, 18 Mansfield Street, London W1M 9FG, tel. 0171 580 5588.

Render, Stucco and Plaster

The Institute of Advanced Architectural Studies, The King's Manor, York YO1 2EP, tel. 01904 433987.

The Lime Centre, Long Barn, Morestead, Winchester, Hants SO21 1LZ, tel. 01962 713636. Runs courses on all aspects of lime production and use.

Tomei & Sons, 42 St John's Road, London SE20 7ED, tel. 0181 778 8928.

National Lime Suppliers

Bleaklow Industries, Hassop Avenue, Hassop, Derbyshire DE45 1NS, tel. 01246 582284.

H.J. Chard & Sons, Albert Road, Bristol BS2 0XS, tel. 0117 977 7681.

Hirst Conservation Materials, Laughton Hall Farmhouse, Laughton, Sleaford, Lincs NG34 0HE, tel. 01529 497517.

The Lime Centre, Long Barn, Morestead, Winchester, Hants SO21 1LZ, tel. 01962 713636.

Potmolen, 27 Woodcock Industrial Estate, Warminster, Wilts BA12 9DX, tel. 01985 213960.

St Blaise Ltd, Westhill Barn, Evershot, Dorchester, Dorset DT2 0LD, tel. 01935 83662. Advice only; for supplies contact Rose of Jericho at the same address.

Totternhoe Lime & Stone Co., Totternhoe, Dunstable, Beds LU6 2BU, tel. 01525 220300.

Windows

The Glass and Glazing Federation, 44-8 Borough High Street, London SE1 1XB, tel. 0171 403 7177.

Sibley & Son, PO Box 271, Woking, Surrey GU22 0YX, tel. 01426 949346.

The Worshipful Company of Glaziers and Painters of Glass, Glaziers' Hall, 9 Montague Close, London Bridge, London SE1 9DD, tel. 0171 403 0330.

Draughtproofing Firms:

Delmae Systems, 4 Ringstead Way, Aylesbury, Bucks HP21 7ND, tel. 01296 394993.

Peter Heywood & Associates Ltd, Unit 1, 44 North Road, Chavey Down, Ascot, Berks SL5 8RP, tel. 01344 424469.

Manton Insulation Ltd, Little End Road, Eaton Socon, Cambs PE19 3JH, tel. 01480 214300.

Mighton Products, PO Box 1, Saffron Walden, Essex CB10 1QJ, tel. 01799 531011.

Sashy & Sashy, 5 Phoenix Lane, Ashurstwood, East Grinstead, West Sussex RH19 3RA, tel. 01342 823408.

Schlegel (UK) Engineering Ltd, Henlow Industrial Estate, Henlow Camp, Beds SG16 6DS, tel. 01462 815500.

Sealmaster Ltd, Brewery Road, Pampisford, Cambs CB2 4HG, tel. 01223 832851.

Slott Seal Ltd: A Division of Stadium Ltd, Fleming Road, Earlstrees Industrial Estate, Corby, Northants NN17 4TY, tel. 01536 200555.

Ventrolla, 51 Tower Street, Harrogate, North Yorks HG1 1HS, tel. 01423 567004.

Traditional Glass Substitutes:

James Hetley & Co. Ltd, Glasshouse Fields, Ratcliffe, London E1 9JA, tel. 0171 790 2333. Imported Georgian glass substitutes.

The London Crown Glass Company, Pyghtle House, Misbourne Avenue, Gerrards Cross, Bucks SL9 0PD, tel. 01497 871966. Agent for new, British-made crown glass and for

imported Georgian glass substitutes.
Benjamin Sinclair, Norgrove Studios, Bentley, Redditch, Worcs B97 5UH, tel. 01527 541545.

Roofs

The Clay Roofing Tile Council, Federation House, Station Road, Stoke-on-Trent, Staffs ST4 2SA, tel. 01782 744631.
The Lead Sheet Association, St John's Road, Tunbridge Wells, Kent TN4 9XA, tel. 01892 513351.
Roofing Tile Association, 60 Charles Street, Leicester LE1 1FB, tel. 0116 253 6161.
The Royal Institution of Chartered Surveyors, 12 Great George Street, London SW1P 3AD, tel. 0171 222 7000. Advice on skilled and independent surveyors.

Ironwork

The British Foundry Association, 8th Floor, Bridge House, Smallbrook Queensway, Birmingham B5 4JP, tel. 0121 643 3377.
The Brooking Collection, University of Greenwich, Oakfield Lane, Dartford, Kent DA1 2SD, tel. 01485 504555. A large, invaluable collection of ironwork from every period; access by appointment only.
Ironbridge Gorge Museum, Ironbridge, Shropshire TF8 7AW, tel. 01952 433522.
The Victoria and Albert Museum, Metalwork, Silver and Jewellery Department, Cromwell Road, South Kensington, London SW7 2RL, tel. 0171 938 8500.

Paint (*Suppliers of Traditional Paints or Paint Colours*)

Brodie & Middleton, 68 Drury Lane, London WC2, tel. 0171 836 3289.
Cole & Son Ltd, 144 Offord Road, London N1 1NS, tel. 0171 607 4288.
Hirst Conservation Materials, Laughton Hall Farmhouse, Laughton, Sleaford, Lincs, NG34 0HE, tel. 01529 497157.
John T. Keep & Son Ltd, 15 Theobald's Road, London WC1, tel. 0171 242 7578.
John Oliver, 33 Pembridge Road, London W11 3HG, tel. 0171 221 6466.
Papers and Paints Ltd, 4 Park Walk, London SW10 0AD, tel. 0171 352 8626.
Potmolen Paint, 27 Woodcock Industrial Estate, Warminster, Wilts BA12 9DX, tel. 01985 213960.
John Sutcliffe, 12 Huntington Road, Cambridge CB3 0HH, tel. 01223 315858.

Wallpaper

Baer & Ingram, 273 Wandsworth Bridge Road, London SW6 2TX, tel. 0171 736 6111. A wide range of historic reproductions from a variety of firms.
Cole & Son Ltd, 144 Offord Road, London N1 1NS, tel. 0171 607 4288. Also own Perrys of Islington, who still handblock papers in the traditional manner.
Colefax & Fowler, 39 Brook Street, London W1Y 2JE, tel. 0171 493 2231.
De Gournay, 14 Hyde Park Gate, London SW7 5DG, tel. 0171 823 7316.
Hamilton Weston, 18 St Mary's Grove, Richmond, Surrey TW9 1UY, tel. 0181 940 4850. Historic reproductions and matching service; also advise on dating and conservation.
Lintz Green Studios, Rowlands Gill, Co. Durham NE39 1NL, tel. 01207 271547.
Orde Solomons, 50 Amersham Road, New Cross, London SE14 6QE, tel. 0181 692 2016. Expert wallpaper removal.
Temple Newsam House, Leeds LS15 0AE, tel. 0113 264 7321.
Zoffany, 63 South Audley Street, London W1Y 5BF, tel. 0171 495 2502. Range includes reproductions of papers found at Temple Newsam.

Curtains, Blinds and Furnishings

Manchester City Council Conservation Studios, Queen's Park, Harpurhey, Manchester M23 0AB, tel. 0161 998 2331. Advice only; not suppliers.
Temple Newsam House, Leeds LS15 0AE, tel. 0113 264 7321.
The Textile Conservation Centre, Apartment 22, Hampton Court Palace, East Molesey, Surrey KT8 9AU, tel. 0181 977 4943. The world's leading centre for the conservation of fabrics; also trains conservationists.
UK Institute for Conservation, 6 Whitehorse Mews, Westminster Bridge Road, London SE1 7QD, tel. 0171 603 5643.
The Victoria and Albert Museum, Department of Furniture and Woodwork, Cromwell Road, South Kensington, London SW7 2RL, tel. 0171 938 8500.

Floor Coverings

Manchester City Council Conservation Studios, Queen's Park, Harpurhey, Manchester M23 0AB, tel. 0161 998 2331. Advice only; not suppliers.

Temple Newsam House, Leeds LS15 0AE, tel. 0113 264 7321. Expert advice on all aspects of the Georgian floor.

The Textile Conservation Centre, Apartment 22, Hampton Court Palace, East Molesey, Surrey KT8 9AU, tel. 0181 977 4943.

Lighting

The Historical Lighting Club (UK), 23 Northcourt Road, Abingdon, Oxon OX14 1PW, tel. 01235 522107.

Temple Newsam House, Leeds LS15 0AE, tel. 0113 264 7321.

The Victoria and Albert Museum, Department of Furniture and Woodwork, Cromwell Road, South Kensington, London SW7 2RL, tel. 0171 938 8500.

Services

Georgian Kitchens Open to the Public

No. 1 Royal Crescent, Bath (reconstructed)

Brighton Pavilion

The Georgian House, Charlotte Street, Bristol

Pickford's House, Friar Gate, Derby (a Late Georgian townhouse kitchen with a range of 1822)

Ecclefechan, Dumfries (Carlisle's birthplace, kitchen of 1791)

Lanhydrock, Cornwall (National Trust)

Powderham Castle, Devon (National Trust)

Saltram, Devon (National Trust)

Wallington, Northumberland (National Trust)

Fairfax House, York (reconstructed)

UNITED STATES

In every state and region of the United States there are numerous suppliers of building and renovation materials ranging from mouldings and fixtures to wallpaper and fabrics. Many of these suppliers carry Georgian-style items, and it is beyond the scope of this book to attempt to list a meaningful number of them in every region of the country. However, it is possible to obtain information about these sources through many of the organizations listed below.

The National Trust for Historic Preservation

The National Trust (1785 Massachusetts Avenue NW, Washington, DC 20036, tel. 202 675 4000) is an invaluable resource, offering advice on repair and maintenance through books published by The Preservation Press, as well as through leaflets, a bimonthly magazine, a monthly newsletter, and a wide range of conferences, seminars and workshops. Advice is available to homeowners through the Trust's regional offices, listed below.

Northeast Regional Office, Seven Faneuil Hall Marketplace, 5th Floor, Boston, MA 02109, tel. 617 523 0885.

Mid-Atlantic Regional Office, One Penn Center at Suburban Station, Suite 1520, 1617 John F. Kennedy Boulevard, Philadelphia, PA 19103-1815, tel. 215 568 8162.

Southern Regional Office, 456 King Street, Charleston, SC 29403, tel. 803 722 8552.

Midwest Regional Office, 53 West Jackson Boulevard, Suite 1135, Chicago, IL 60604, tel. 312 939 5547.

Mountain Plains Regional Office, 910 16th Street, Suite 1100, Denver, CO 80202, tel. 303 623 1504.

Western Regional Office, One Sutter Street, Suite 707, San Francisco, CA 94104, tel. 415 956 0610.

Texas/New Mexico Field Office, 500 Main Street, Suite 606, Fort Worth, TX 76102, tel. 817 332 4398.

Other Useful Addresses

The Historic American Buildings Survey, The Division of Prints and Photographs, Library of Congress, Washington, DC 20540, tel. 205 707 6394. This organization maintains a large collection of photographs, drawings, and documents relating to many houses nationwide.

The Society for Architectural Historians, 1232 Pine Street, Philadelphia, PA 19107, tel. 215

735 0224. The AHSS, the national academic society for architectural history, offers information through its publications, local events and seminars, as well as its annual conference.

The American Society of Interior Designers, 608 Massachusetts Avenue NE, Washington, DC 20002, tel. 202 546 3480.

The Antiquarian and Landmarks Society, 394 Main Street, Hartford, CT 06103, tel. 203 247 8996.

National Preservation Institute, National Building Museum, 401 F. Street NW, Washington, DC 20001, tel. 202 272 2448.

The American Association for State and Local History, 172 2nd Avenue, North Suite 202, Nashville, TN 37201, tel. 615 255 2971.

The Society for the Preservation of New England Antiquities, 141 Cambridge Street, Boston, MA 02114, tel. 617 227 3956.

Museums with Collections that Pertain to the Period

Colonial Williamsburg, Williamsburg, VA 23187, tel. 804 220 7645.

Cooper-Hewitt National Museum of Design, 2 East 91 Street, New York, NY 10128, tel. 212 860 6898.

Essex Institute, 132 Essex Street, Salem, MA 01970, tel. 508 745 1876.

Henry Francis Du Pont Winterthur Museum, Route 52, Winterthur, DE 19735, tel. 302 888 4600.

Metropolitan Museum of Art, 5th Avenue, New York, NY 10028, tel. 212 535 7710.

Museum of American Textile History, 800 Massachusetts Avenue, North Andover, MA 01845, tel. 508 686 0191.

Museum of Early Southern Decorative Arts, P.O. Box 10310, Winston Salem, NC 27108, tel. 910 721 7360.

Museum of Fine Arts, 4665 Huntington Avenue, Boston, MA 02115, tel. 617 267 9300.

Philadelphia Museum of Art, 26th Street, Philadelphia, PA 19130, tel. 215 763 8100.

Rhode Island School of Design Museum of Art, 224 Benefit Street, Providence, RI 02903, tel. 401 454 6500.

The Textile Museum, 2320 S Street NW, Washington, DC 20008, tel. 202 667 0441.

Further Reading

[*available from US only]

CHAPTERS 1-5:
THE GEORGIAN HOUSE

Robert Adam, *Classical Architecture* (Viking, 1990)

*Advisory Council on Historic Preservation, *Preservation and Conservation: Principles and Practices* (The Preservation Press, 1976)

Colin Amery, ed, *Period Houses and their Details* (Butterworth, 1978)

John and Nicola Ashurst, *Practical Building Conservation* (English Heritage, 1988, 5 vols)

*John Burns, ed, *Recording Historic Structures* (AIA Press, 1898)

Robert Chitham, *The Classical Orders of Architecture* (Butterworth, 1985)

Cramsay and Harvey, *Small Georgian Houses and Their Details* (Butterworth, 1977)

Dan Cruickshank, *A Guide to the Georgian Buildings of Britain and Ireland* (Weidenfeld & Nicolson, 1985)

Dan Cruickshank and Neil Burton, *Life in the Georgian City* (Viking Penguin, 1990)

Davey, Heath et al, eds, *The Care and Conservation of Georgian Houses* (Butterworth, 3rd ed, 1986)

*Charles E. Fisher *The Interiors Handbook for Historic Buildings* (Historic Preservation Education Foundation, 1988)

*Stephen George, *New Life for Old Houses* (The Preservation Press, 1989)

Eileen Harris, *British Architectural Books and Writers 1556–1785* (CUP, 1990)

*Gary Hume and W. Brown Morton, *Standards for Historic Preservation Projects* (US Dept of the Interior, 1990)

*Judith L. Kitchen, *Caring for Your Old House* (The Preservation Press, 1991)

Nathaniel Lloyd, *A History of the English House* (Architectural Press, 1931)

*National Parks Service, *Respectful Rehabilitation* (The Preservation Press, 1982)

Steven Parissien, *Adam Style* (Phaidon/The Preservation Press, 1992)

Steven Parissien, *Palladian Style* (Phaidon, 1994)

Steven Parissien, *Regency Style* (Phaidon/The Preservation Press, 1992)

*Stephen J. Phillips, *The Old-House Dictionary* (The Preservation Press, 1992)

A. R. Powys, *The Repair of Ancient Buildings* (SPAB, 1929)

Matthew Saunders, *The Historic Home Owner's Companion* (Batsford, 1987)

*Stanley Schuler, *Architectural Details of Old New England Homes* (Schiffer, 1987)

Gavin Stamp, 'Origins of the [Georgian] Group' in *The Architect's Journal*, 31 March 1982

Peter Thornton, *Authentic Decor: The Domestic Interior 1620–1920* (Weidenfeld & Nicolson, 1984)

Marcus Whiffen, *American Architecture Since 1780* (MIT Press, 1981)

CHAPTER 6: BRICKWORK

John and Nicola Ashurst, *Practical Building Conservation*, vol.2: *Terracotta, Brick and Earth* (English Heritage, 1988)

M. W. Barley, *The English Farmhouse and Cottage* (1961)

R. W. Brunskill, *Brick Building in Britain* (Gollancz, 1990)

Alan Cox, *Brickmaking* (Bedfordshire CC, 1979)

Robert Hayward, *The Brick Book* (1978)

Nathaniel Lloyd, *A History of English Brickwork* (1925/1983)

Gerard Lynch, *Brickwork* (Donhead, 1994)

W. G. Nash, *Brickwork Repair and Restoration* (Eastbourne, 1985)

*National Park Service, *Repointing Mortar Joints in Historic Buildings* (US Dept of the Interior, Preservation Brief no.2)

Tunstall Small and Christopher Woodbridge, *English Brickwork Details 1450–1750* (Architectural Press, 1920)

John Woodforde, *Bricks to Build a House* (Routledge, Kegan Paul, 1976)

CHAPTER 7: STONEWORK

John and Nicola Ashurst, *Practical Building Conservation*, vol.1: *Stone Masonry* (English Heritage, 1988)

John and Nicola Ashurst, *Cleaning Stone and Brick* (SPAB Technical Pamphlet 4, 1977)

Nicola Ashurst, *Cleaning* (Donhead, 1994)

A. and M. Caroe, *Stonework: Maintenance and Surface Repair* (CIO, 1984)

Alec Clifton-Taylor, *The Pattern of English Building* (Batsford, 1962)

Alec Clifton-Taylor and A.S. Ireson, *English Stone Building* (Gollancz, 1983)

Pamela Cunnington, *Care for Old Houses* (A. & C. Black, 2nd ed, 1991)

Bruce and Liz Induni, *Using Lime* (SPAB, 1990)

The Natural Stone Directory (Ealing Publications, 1985)

E. Leary, *The Building Limestones of the British Isles* (HMSO, 1983)

E. Leary, *The Building Sandstones of the British Isles* (HMSO, 1986)

*Mark London, *Masonry: How to Care for Old and Historic Brick and Stone* (The Preservation Press, 1988)

Walter Shepherd, *Flint: Its Origins, Properties and Uses* (Faber, 1972)

Andrew Thomas, *The Treatment of Damp in Old Buildings* (SPAB Technical Pamphlet 8, 1986)

Gilbert Williams and Nicola Ashurst, *An Introduction to the Treatment of Damp* (SPAB Information Sheet 6, 1987)

Gilbert Williams, *Pointing Brick and Stone Walling* (SPAB Technical Pamphlet 5, 1986)

Adela Wright, *Craft Techniques for Traditional Buildings* (Batsford, 1991)

Adela Wright, *Removing Paint from Old Buildings* (SPAB Information Sheet 5, 1986)

CHAPTER 8: RENDER AND STUCCO

John Ashurst, *Practical Building Conservation*, vol. 3: *Mortars, Plasters and Renders* (English Heritage, 1988)

John Fidler, 'A Good Rendering' in *Traditional Homes*, March 1992

Philip Hughes, *The Need for Old Buildings to Breathe* (SPAB Information Sheet 4)

Alison Kelly, *Mrs Coade's Stone* (Self-Publishing Association, 1990)

Frank Kelsall, 'Liardet Versus Adam' in *Architectural History*, vol.27, 1984 and 'Stucco' in Hobhouse and Sanders, eds, *Good and Proper Materials* (London Topographical Society, 1989)

*National Park Service, *The Preservation and Repair of Historic Stucco* (US Dept of the Interior, Preservation Brief no.22)

Jane Schofield, *Basic Limewash* (SPAB Information Sheet)

Andrew Townsend, *Roughcast for Historic Buildings* (SPAB Information Sheet 11)

CHAPTER 9: WEATHERBOARDING

*National Park Service, *Aluminium and Vinyl Siding on Historic Buildings* and *External Paint Problems on Historic Woodwork* (US Dept of the Interior, Preservation Briefs nos 8 & 10)

CHAPTER 10: WINDOWS

Dan Cruickshank and Peter Wyld, *London: The Art of Georgian Building* (Architectural Press, 1975)

R. W. Douglas and S. Frank, *A History of Glassmaking* (1972)

English Heritage, *Sash Windows* (EH Advice Leaflet, 1989)

*Charles Fisher, ed, *The Window Workbook for Historic Buildings* (Historic Preservation Education Foundation, 1986)

*National Park Service, *The Repair of Historic Wooden Windows* (US Dept of the Interior, Preservation Brief no.9)

Andrew Townsend and Martin Clarke, *The Repair of Timber Windows* (SPAB Technical Pamphlet No.13, 1991)

UPVC Windows: The Facts (Northern Consortium of Housing Authorities, 1990)

CHAPTER 11: DOORS

Colin Amery, *Three Centuries of Architectural Craftsmanship* (Butterworth, 1986)

Andrew Byrne, *Bedford Square* (Athlone, 1990)

Dan Cruickshank and Peter Wyld, *London: The Art of Georgian Building* (Architectural Press, 1975)

W. G. Davie and G. Tanner, *Old English Doorways* (1903)

J. S. Gray, John Sambrook and Charlotte Halliday, *Fanlights* (A. & C. Black, 1989)

CHAPTER 12: ROOFS

M. A. Aston, *Stonesfield Slate* (Oxon Museums Service, 1974)

F. Bennett, *Roof Tiling and Slating* (1935)

James Boutwood, *The Repair of Timber Frames and Roofs* (SPAB Technical Pamphlet 12)

Christopher Brereton, *The Repair of Historic Buildings* (English Heritage, 1991)

Peter Brockett and Adela Wright, *The Care and Repair of Thatched Roofs* (SPAB Technical Pamphlet 10)

Alec Clifton-Taylor, *The Pattern of English Building* (Batsford, 1962)

Alec Clifton-Taylor and A. S. Ireson, *English Stone Building* (Gollancz, 1983)

Pamela Cunnington, *Care for Old Houses* (A. & C. Black, 2nd ed, 1991)

C. Dobson, *Slating and Tiling* (Langley, 1957)

English Heritage, *Mansard Roofs* (EH Guidance Leaflet, 1990)

John Fidler, 'Roof Recognition', in *Traditional Homes* February/April 1985 and 'Plumbing the Heights' in *Traditional Homes*, September 1992

Tony Herbert, 'Roofs of Clay' in *Traditional Homes*, February 1988

Lead Development Association, *Lead Sheet in Building* (1978)

*National Parks Service, *Roofing for Historic Buildings* and *The Repair and Replacement of Historic Wooden Shingle Roofs* (US Dept of the Interior, Preservation Briefs nos 4 & 19)

P. M. Sutton-Gould, *Decorative Leadwork* (Shire, 1990)

Michael Thornton, *Traditional Homes* articles: 'Curved Cover-Up' (clay pantiles), December 1988; 'Perfectly Plain' (repairing plain tiles), February 1989; 'Lessons on Slates', March/April 1989; 'A Choice of Channels' (guttering), June 1989

Laurence Weaver, *English Leadwork* (1909)

G. B. A. Williams, *Chimneys in Old Buildings* (SPAB Technical Pamphlet 3)

Adela Wright, *Craft Techniques for Traditional Buildings* (Batsford, 1991)

CHAPTER 13: IRONWORK

John and Nicola Ashurst, *Practical Building Conservation*, vol 4: *Metals* (English Heritage, 1988)

Amina Chatwin, *Cheltenham's Ornamental Ironwork* (self-published, 1975)

Edward Diestelkamp, 'Building Technology and Architecture 1790–1830' in White and Lightburn, eds, *Late Georgian Classicism* (The Georgian Group, 1988)

Jacqueline Fearn, *Cast Iron* (Shire, 1990)

John Gay, *Cast Iron Architecture and Ornament* (1985)

*Margot Gayle etc, *Metals in America's Historic Buildings* (US Dept of the Interior, 1980)

*Anne E. Grimmer, *Keeping It Clean* (US Dept of the Interior, 1988)

John Harris, *The British Iron Industry 1700–1850* (1988)

The Iron Revolution (RIBA catalogue, 1990)

Lindsay Seymour, *Iron and Brass Implements of the English House* (1988)

D. S. Waite, *Ornamental Ironwork* (1990)

Suggested Georgian Pattern-Books:

Robert and James Adam, *Works in Architecture* (1774)

L. N. Cottingham, *The Smith and Founder's Director* (1823)

J. C. Loudon, *An Encyclopaedia of Villa, Farm and Cottage Architecture* (1833)

Peter Nicholson, *Mechanical Exercises* (1812)

Henry Shaw, *Examples of Ornamental Metalwork* (1836)

W. and J. Welldon, *The Smith's Right Hand* (1745 and 1765)

CHAPTER 14: MOULDINGS

Dan Cruickshank, 'Material Success' in *Renovation (AJ Supplement)*, March 1989 *Moldings* (The Preservation Press)

Franz Meyer, *Handbook of Ornament* (Batsford, 1888)

Tunstall Small and Christopher Woodbridge, *Houses of the Wren and Georgian Periods* (Architectural Press, 1932)

Suggested Georgian Pattern-Books:

James Gibbs, *Rules for Drawing* (1732)

Joseph Gwilt, *An Encyclopaedia of Architecture* (1842)

William Halfpenny, *The Art of Sound Building* (1723)

William Halfpenny, *Practical Architecture* (1736)

Batty Langley, *The Builder's Complete Assistant* (1738)

Batty Langley, *The Builder's Director* (1747) (also numerous other useful volumes by Batty Langley)

Peter Nicholson, *Mechanical Exercises* (1812)

Peter Nicholson, *An Architectural Dictionary* (1819)

William Pain, *The Carpenter's and Joiner's Repository* (1778)

William Pain, *The Practical House Carpenter* (1789)

Abraham Swan, *A Collection of Designs in Architecture* (1757)

CHAPTER 15: FLOORS

John Fidler, 'Dirty Business' (floor cleaning) in *Traditional Homes*, June 1986

Christopher Gilbert, James Lomax and Anthony Wells-Cole, *Country House Floors*

FURTHER READING

(Leeds City Art Galleries, 1987)
Philip Hughes, *Patching Old Floorboards* (SPAB Information Sheet 10, 1988)
John Macgregor, *Strengthening Timber Floors* (SPAB Technical Pamphlet 2, 1985)
Rosalind Pilling, 'Wooden Floors in Evolution' in *Traditional Homes*, February 1987
Hermione Sandwith and Sheila Stainton, *The National Trust Manual of Housekeeping* (The National Trust, 2nd ed, 1990)

CHAPTER 16: STAIRCASES

Peter Nicholson, *Treatise on the Construction of Staircases* (1820)
Tunstall Small and Christopher Woodbridge, *Architectural Turned Woodwork of the 16th, 17th and 18th Centuries* (Architectural Press, 1926)
Abraham Swan, *The British Architect* (1745)
W. and J. Welldon, *The Smith's Right Hand* (1745 and 1765)

CHAPTER 17: FIREPLACES

Pauline Agius, ed, *Ackermann's Furniture and Interiors* (Cameron, 1984)
David Eveleigh, *Firegrates and Kitchen Ranges* (Shire, 1983)
Jacqueline Fearn, *Cast Iron* (Shire, 1990)
Christopher Gilbert and Anthony Wells-Cole, *The Fashionable Fire Place* (Leeds City Galleries, 1985)
Nicholas Hills, *The English Fireplace* (Quiller, 1983)
Alison Kelly, *The Book of English Fireplaces* (Country Life, 1968)
Roxana McDonald, *The Fireplace Book* (Architectural Press, 1984)

Suggested Georgian Pattern-Books:
Robert and James Adam, *Works in Architecture* (1774)
William Chambers, *Treatise* (1759)
James Gibbs, *Rules of Drawing* (1732)
William Glossop, *The Stove-Grate Maker's Assistant* (1771)
William and John Halfpenny: various works, from *Practical Architecture* (1724) to *The Country Gentleman's Pocket Companion and Builder's Assistant* (1753–6)
William Kent, *Designs of Inigo Jones, with some Additional Designs* (1737)
Batty Langley: various works, from *A Sure Guide to Builders* (1729) to *The Builder's Director* (1747)
J. C. Loudon, *An Encyclopaedia of Villa, Farm and Cottage Architecture* (1833)

James Paine, *Plans, Sections and Elevations of Noblemen's and Gentlemen's Houses* (1767)
John Vardy, *The Works of Mr Inigo Jones and Mr William Kent* (1744)
W. and J. Welldon, *The Smith's Right Hand* (1765 ed.)

CHAPTER 18: PLASTER

John and Nicola Ashurst, *Practical Building Conservation*, vol.3: *Mortars, Plasters and Renders* (English Heritage, 1988)
George Bankhart, *The Art of the Plasterer* (1910)
Geoffery Beard, *Decorative Plasterwork in Great Britain* (1975)
Geoffrey Beard, *Craftsmen and Interior Decoration in England 1660–1820* (John Bartholomew, 1981)
John Fidler, 'Save the Ceiling' in *Traditional Homes*, March 1986
Philip Hughes, *The Need for Old Buildings to Breathe* (SPAB Information Sheet 1)
Frank Kelsall, 'Stucco' in *Good and Proper Materials* (London Topographical Society, 1989)
William Miller, *Plaster Plain and Decorative* (1899)
*National Parks Service, *Repairing Historic Flat Plaster* and *Preserving Historic Ornamental Plaster* (US Dept of the Interior, Preservation Briefs nos 21 & 23)
Pegg and Stagg, *Plastering – A Craftsman's Encyclopaedia* (1927)
Arnold Root, 'Decorative Plaster Design and Repair' in *Renovation (AJ Supplement)*, March 1989
*Natalie Shivers, *Walls and Molding* (Preservation Press, 1990)
Laurence Turner, *Decorative Plasterwork* (Country Life, 1927)

CHAPTER 19: PAINT COLOUR

Patrick Baty, 'Palette of Historic Paints' in *Country Life*, 20 February 1992 and 'Palette of the Past' in *Country Life*, 2 September 1992
Ian Bristow, 'The Role of Taste' in *Traditional Interior Decoration*, Spring 1986
Ian Bristow and Mark Girouard, eds, *The Saving of Spitalfields* (Spitalfields Trust, 1989)
Edward Croft-Murray, *Decorative Painting in England* (Thames & Hudson, 1962–70)
John Fowler and John Cornforth, *English Decoration in the 18th Century* (Barrie & Jenkins, 1978)
Charlotte Gere, *Nineteenth Century Decoration* (Weidenfeld & Nicolson, 1989)

*Kevin H. Miller, ed, *Paint Colour Research and Restoration of Historic Paint* (Association for Preservation Technology (Canada), 1977)

CHAPTER 20: WALLPAPERS
Phyllis Ackerman, *Wallpaper* (Heinemann, 1923)

E. A. Entwisle, *The Book of Wallpaper* (Arthur Barker, 1954)

*Catherine Lynn Frangiamore, *Wallpapers in Historic Preservation* (US Dept of the Interior, 1977)

Allyson McDermott, 'Decorative Discoveries' in *Traditional Homes*, August 1987

*Odile Nouvel, *Wallpapers of France 1800–1850* (Rizzoli, 1981)

*Richard C. Nylander, *Wallpapers for Historic Buildings* (The Preservation Press, 1983)

*Richard C. Nylander ed, *Wallpapers in New England* (Society for the Preservation of New England Antiquities, 1986)

Charles Oman and Jean Hamilton, *Wallpapers* (Thames & Hudson, 1982)

Treve Rosoman, *London Wallpapers – their manufacture and use 1690–1840* (English Heritage, 1992)

A. V. Sugden and J. L. Edmondson, *A History of English Wallpaper* (1926)

Anthony Wells-Cole, *Historic Paper Hangings* (Leeds City Art Galleries, 1983)

CHAPTER 21: CURTAINS, SHUTTERS AND BLINDS
Pauline Agius, ed, *Ackermann's Furniture and Interiors* (Cameron Press, 1984)

Christopher Gilbert, *The Life and Work of Thomas Chippendale* (Studio Editions, 1978)

Clare Jameson, ed, *A Pictorial Treasury of Curtain and Drapery Designs 1750–1850* (Potterton, 1987)

J. C. Loudon, *The Encyclopaedia of Cottage, Farm and Villa Architecture* (1833)

*Florence Montgomery, *Textiles in America* (W. W. Norton, 1984)

*Jane C. Nylander, *Fabrics for Historic Buildings* (The Preservation Press, 4th ed, 1990)

Treve Rosoman, 'Swags and Festoons' in *Traditional Interior Decoration*, Autumn 1986 and 'In the Shade' in *Traditional Homes*, July 1985

Hermione Sandwith and Sheila Stainton, *The National Trust Manual of Housekeeping* (The National Trust, 2nd ed, 1990)

Mary Schoeser and Celia Rufey, *English and American Textiles: 1790 to the Present Day* (Thames & Hudson, 1989)

CHAPTER 22: FLOOR COVERINGS
James Ayres, 'Simple Floors and Floor Coverings' in *Traditional Homes*, June–August 1985

Ian Bristow, 'Painted Floorcloths in the 18th Century' in *SPAB News*, vol.11 no.2, 1990

Christopher Gilbert, James Lomax and Anthony Wells-Cole, *Country House Floors* (Leeds City Art Galleries, 1987)

*Helene von Rosensteil and Gail Winkler, *Floor Coverings for Historic Buildings* (The Preservation Press, 1988)

CHAPTER 23: LIGHTING
Jonathan Bourne and Vanessa Brett, *Lighting* (Sothebys, 1991)

Christopher Gilbert, Anthony Wells-Cole etc, *Country House Lighting* (Leeds City Art Galleries, 1992)

Arthur H. Hayward, *Colonial Lighting* (1927, reprinted by Dover 1962)

Alastair Laing, *Lighting* (V&A exhibition catalogue, 1982)

*Roger W. Moss, *Lighting for Historic Buildings* (The Preservation Press, 1988)

Hermione Sandwith and Sheila Stainton, *The National Trust Manual of Housekeeping* (The National Trust, 2nd ed, 1990)

Index

PICTURE CREDITS

All photographs are the author's, except on the following pages:

Ian Parry: Frontispiece, 10, 13, 18, 19, 23, 25, 26, 27, 29, 31, 42, 45, 46, 50–1, 52, 54, 64, 74, 82, 90, 94-5, 99, 101, 102, 106, 108, 110, 121, 126, 127, 130, 132, 134–5, 138, 142, 146, 148, 149, 150, 151, 154, 158, 159, 162, 163, 166, 169, 170, 171, 174, 175, 176, 181, 182, 183, 192,1 93, 206, 218, 222, 223, 226, 227; The Bristol Architectural Library/RIBA: 156, 225; The British Library: 20, 21, 28, 140, 224; Coles & Son: 188; Edinburgh New Town Conservation Committee/Butterworths: 105, 161; English Heritage: 18, 160; The Georgian Group: 14 bottom, 201; De Gournay: 186; Gunston Hall, Virginia: 35; The Hammond-Harwood House, Annapolis, Maryland: 111; Hayles & Howe Ltd: 168 right; Tony Herbert: 157; Historic Buildings Services Ltd: 115; The Hon. Simon Howard: 168 left; Kenmore, Virginia: 167; Iain McCaig: 60, 63, 64; Massachusetts Historical Society: 38; Monticello, Virginia: 39; Mount Vernon: 37, 143, 213, 215; The National Gallery of Ireland: 178, 190; Northern Virginia Regional Park Authority: 177; Treve Rosoman: 165; The Royal Collection, St James' Palace, © HM The Queen: 198; Syon House, Middlesex: 210; The Board of Trustees of the Victoria and Albert Museum: 211, 213, 216; Rory Young: 79.

Thanks are also due to Christopher Woodward and The Building of Bath Museum for permission to photograph the museum exhibits; to Patrick Baty for his invaluable assistance on the photography of historic paints; Karin Walton and Bristol Museums and Art Gallery for permission to photograph the Georgian House in Bristol; to Charles Brooking for permission to photograph items from The Brooking Collection; The National Trust for permission to photograph at Osterley Park; John Cordle and the late Sir Philip Shelbourne for permission to photograph their Salisbury homes; Christopher Gilbert, Adam White and the staff at Temple Newsam, Leeds, for permission to photograph the house's contents and their help with the text; Duncan Wilson and Dan Cruickshank for permission to photograph their London homes; and to Julia B. Claypool of the Carlyle House, Alexandria, the Northern Virginia Regional Park Authority, and Stephen B. Patrick of the Hammond-Harwood House, Annapolis, for kindly providing illustrations of their respective houses.